Turning BEST Practices into DAILY Practices

Simple Strategies for the Busy Teacher

Anne M. Beninghof

Crystal Springs
SDE BOOKS

a division of Staff Development for Educators
Peterborough, New Hampshire

Acknowledgments

Thank you, thank you, thank you to all the teachers who have so generously shared ideas with me. Special thanks to Alicia, Barb, Grace, and Lora for welcoming me with open arms into your dynamic learning community. You are truly inspiring!

Published by Crystal Springs Books
A division of Staff Development for Educators (SDE)
10 Sharon Road, PO Box 500
Peterborough, NH 03458
1-800-321-0401
www.sde.com/crystalsprings

© 2010 Anne M. Beninghof
Illustrations © 2010 Crystal Springs Books

Published 2010
Printed in the United States of America
14   4 5

ISBN: 978-1-934026-60-1

Library of Congress Cataloging-in-Publication Data

Beninghof, Anne M.
  Turning best practices into daily practices : simple strategies for the busy teacher / Anne M. Beninghof.
      p. cm.
  Includes bibliographical references and index.
  ISBN 978-1-934026-60-1
  1. Teaching--Aids and devices. 2. Effective teaching. I. Title.

  LB1044.88.B46 2009
  371.102--dc22

                                                          2009022602

Editor: Sharon Smith
Art Director and Designer: Soosen Dunholter
Production Coordinator: Deborah Fredericks
Illustrator: Joyce Rainville

Contents

Fourth Quarter

Introduction

In recent years, the U.S. Patent and Trademark Office has received more than 400,000 patent applications annually. The role of the patent office is to promote the progress of science and the useful arts by securing exclusive rights for inventors. According to law, something worthy of a patent must be "useful." While the determination of "useful" is complicated and contentious, it is clear that Americans have invented many wonderful, useful things.

At the Web site of the National Inventors Hall of Fame you can find tributes to hundreds of acclaimed inventors and successful inventions. Milton Bradley invented the Checkered Game of Life (Patent #53,561), the first patented board game. During the Civil War, Bradley recognized that the spirits of the American people needed a lift. He conceived of a game that could bring joy and knowledge to young and old alike. He designed a board with a spinner and sold 40,000 copies in the first year. The game is still popular today.

John Kellogg invented Corn Flakes (Patent #558,393), the first dry, flaked breakfast cereal in the world. Accident led to this discovery—Kellogg was working for a sanitarium, experimenting with new food products. He rolled out some wheat dough that had accidentally been left out overnight and found that instead of making loaves of bread, it made thin wheat flakes. With rave reviews from patients at the sanitarium, and a few changes, Corn Flakes became an instant success.

Laszlo Biro invented the modern ballpoint pen (Patent #2,390,636). Biro, a journalist, was tired of the ink from his fountain pen leaving notes that were easily smudged. He tried printing-press ink, but found it too thick to flow through the tip of a fountain pen. Then he tried placing a small, rotating ball in the tip of the pen. That addition allowed the thicker ink to be picked up from a reservoir and placed on the page. His invention was first applied in the airplane indus-

> He rolled out some wheat dough that had accidentally been left out overnight and found that instead of making loaves of bread, it made thin wheat flakes.

try, where air pressure negatively affected the flow of ink in fountain pens. Today, ballpoint pens are used in every walk of life.

The usefulness of some inventions, however, seems questionable. Consider the black highlighter, the left-handed pencil, the waterproof tea bag, the inflatable dartboard, or the Braille driver's manual. Some apparently useless inventions even get approval from the patent office. Does anyone really need an alarm-equipped fork to indicate that you are eating too quickly or too slowly? Or a courting glove that allows two people to hold hands inside of one glove?

> Does anyone really need an alarm-equipped fork to indicate that you are eating too quickly or too slowly?

In fact, while approximately 50% of patent applications are approved each year, it is estimated that only 1% of new ideas actually result in successful product launches. Why so few? Because having a good idea isn't enough. A successful idea has to meet a clear, common need; save time or money for consumers; and be practical enough to survive in a crowded, competitive market.

Current Initiatives in Education

Educators also see a wide variety of new ideas introduced each year. Our profession has a reputation for continuously seeking out the best ways to improve student learning, and occasionally school systems embrace new ideas without considering their viability over time. Those are the instances in which finding a potential solution seems to have greater appeal than spending time vetting the new idea against some critical criteria first. To guard against that, it might be helpful to evaluate any new ideas in terms of criteria such as these:

- Is the idea supported by research? Scientific research? Action research?
- Is the idea practical enough in terms of money and time for educators to implement it?
- Does the idea pass the commonsense test?
- Is the idea appealing to all involved? Does it bring joy? Satisfaction? Increased motivation?
- Does the idea spark new creation? Does it allow for teacher buy-in through personal adaptation?

Many of the current initiatives in education meet these criteria, and teachers are enthusiastically embracing these ideas as viable ways to improve their teaching. The following developments in education are among those that meet these criteria and share a common, laudable objective of improving learning outcomes for students.

> Teachers build a safe environment in which to share their personal practices, analyze strengths and weaknesses, admit their struggles, and tap into the collective creativity and wisdom of their colleagues.

Professional Learning Communities

Professional Learning Communities (PLCs) are small groups of educators who are committed to continuously seeking out new learning, sharing their experiences, and acting on what they learn. Sometimes these groups are referred to as Process Learning Circles or Communities of Continuous Inquiry and Improvement. But no matter what the groups are called, the goal of this approach to staff development is to enhance teaching effectiveness so that students benefit. Through the small-group structure, teachers build a safe environment in which to share their personal practices, analyze strengths and weaknesses, admit their struggles, and tap into the collective creativity and wisdom of their colleagues. Research shows that teachers who feel supported in their own ongoing learning and practice are more committed to the profession and more effective with students.

Inclusion

Inclusion is both an educational philosophy and a practice. As a philosophy or belief system, inclusion might be defined as recognizing our universal oneness and interdependence. While originally associated with including people with disabilities, the term *inclusion* is now used in connection with all groups of people who might have been excluded previously. In educational circles, inclusion is based on the belief that all children should be valued equally. As a practice, this means that students with disabilities, English Language Learners, or others who traditionally might have been sent down the hall are now considered full members of the general education classroom from the beginning. Necessary support services are brought to the child in the classroom, rather than removing the child to take him to the support services.

Benefits of inclusion are plentiful for students and staff. Inclusive classrooms teach all students that each person has unique talents and gifts to offer the community, that diversity is necessary for a successful society, and that interdependence is as valuable as independence. Struggling students benefit from appropriate role models, higher expectations, greater accountability, and a wider range of resources. Staff benefit from working more closely with colleagues, broadening their perspectives on student abilities, and acquiring teaching strategies that can work for students without labels.

Universal Design

Universal design, a concept that originated in the architectural field, is based on the belief that human abilities are naturally very diverse. With this belief in mind, universal design incorporates accessibility for a wide range of users into any design process right from the beginning, rather than modifying components after the fact. When applied to education, this paradigm shift means viewing individual student differences as natural, rather than problematic.

Universal Design for Learning (UDL) is an approach that applies this belief to classroom practice. The three primary principles that form the structure for UDL require the teacher to plan for multiple means of representation, expression, and engagement. Using technology as an over-arching tool, universal design ensures that lessons are accessible to all students throughout the learning cycle. Information may be represented in a variety of ways (such as video, small-group discussion, and print) and students may express their understanding in a variety of ways (such as models, reports, and media presentations), leading to increased student engagement in the entire process. But UDL goes even further, including adaptations such as flexible font size, varied speeds of audio recordings, the use of partially completed notes—whatever is necessary to make the lesson accessible to all.

> This paradigm shift means viewing individual student differences as natural, rather than problematic.

Differentiated Instruction

Differentiated Instruction (DI) conjures up many images for teachers. Generally, differentiation involves consideration of student interests, learning preferences, and readiness levels across the curriculum. Differentiation can be applied to content, process, and products. It may come into play in one or more parts of the learning cycle, and it often involves simple strategies that allow for greater participation. These DI strategies may be integrated into the original lesson design, or they may be added as the teacher becomes aware of specific needs.

Response to Intervention

Response to Intervention (RTI) is a process for making instructional decisions about struggling students without applying disability labels. It is based on the understanding that curriculum and instructional methods that are effective for one student may not be effective for another student. Once screening assessments have identified a student as struggling, a school can use the RTI framework to support that student with supplemental, research-based instruction and interventions, tiered by increasing levels

> The RTI structure lends itself to assisting students who struggle in reading or in any of the curricular areas, whether or not they are likely to have a disability.

of intensity and duration. The process incorporates collaborative problem-solving and decision making based on data from frequent monitoring of student progress.

RTI is often used as a process for identifying learning disabilities. Interventions occur initially in the classroom, but can lead to pull-out programs with different materials. The RTI structure lends itself to assisting students who struggle in reading or in any of the curricular areas, whether or not they are likely to have a disability. It makes common sense that if a teacher found a student struggling with the material, she would collect key data, adapt her teaching for the individual, and monitor the outcome. Doing this as part of a collaborative, collegial group provides vital support for the teacher and can lead to a more successful outcome for the student.

Putting It All Together

It is exciting to see that the educational developments described above are taking hold in schools all around the country. Teachers are embracing collaborative, inclusive approaches that are resulting in improved student outcomes. From these developments we are seeing a rapid growth in classroom-level applications. But with so many new ideas emerging each year, and so little time to explore them all, teachers need resources that synthesize important new information in a user-friendly format. That is the goal of this book—to take current best practices and help teachers turn them into usable daily practices. A secondary goal is to offer a format for reflective practice, whether on your own or with a group of colleagues. I hope that reflection on these ideas will add to the collective wisdom of teachers everywhere and lead to improved learning for all students.

To determine which best practices to include, I combined an extensive review of the research on effective instructional practices with the voices of practicing teachers, always with the goal of addressing what teachers want. From that synthesis, the following categories of best practices arose:

- Increasing Participation
- Focusing Attention
- Identifying Similarities & Differences
- Using Non-Linguistic Representations

- Making Connections
- Determining Importance
- Strengthening Memory
- Summarizing
- Challenging Thinking

Those are the categories on which I have chosen to focus. This book presents each category separately, but there is a great deal of crossover. For example, it is impossible to make connections without simultaneously strengthening memory, or to summarize without determining importance. Read through the strategies with these interrelationships in mind, and you are bound to make additional connections.

How to Use This Book

The range of research and ideas that support each of these best practices is vast. To organize the information into a teacher-friendly format, I have divided this book into four parts, just as a school year is divided into quarters. Each part includes all nine best practices, just as a school quarter typically encompasses nine weeks. Each of the nine best practices, or weeks, presents one "daily practice" or practical application for you to try that week. Not too overwhelming! For each week, the format flows like this:

Best Practice—one of the nine categories, with research or related literature highlights. This brief review provides supporting evidence and key issues for consideration.

Reflective Questions—three questions for self-reflection based on the research. Linked to the best practice, these three questions will spark your thinking about your personal experiences, your students' experiences, and areas for application.

Idea for Daily Practice—a practical application to try in the classroom. This includes a list of necessary materials and step-by-step directions to ensure that the strategy is implemented successfully. As a bonus, variations are suggested for each daily practice, resulting in a multitude of useful ideas.

Reflections—questions for reflection based on your experience with the strategy. These questions provide you the opportunity to review your success and create potent new strategies.

The format continues until all nine best practices have been presented (following the structure of a typical nine-week quarter) and then begins again. Each quarter of the book reviews the best practices from a distinct perspective, including different research, and provides new daily practices to try. All in all, 36 unique teaching ideas are presented, each including flexible variations—enough to keep you energized throughout the entire school year!

Of course, there is no rule that says you have to progress through the book in sequence. You may decide to identify your instructional objective for a lesson, then search the table of contents or the reference chart on page 12 to find a strategy that is a perfect match. Or you may prefer just to flip open the book and try whatever idea is in front of you. I hope you will feel free to use this book in whatever way works best for you.

> This book lends itself easily to a book discussion because of the structured opportunities for reflection and idea generation.

Book Discussion Groups

In recent years, many teachers have chosen to engage in stimulating dialogue with their colleagues through book discussion groups. Such groups offer a wonderful way to explore the professional literature and broaden understanding of material by sharing a variety of perspectives and experiences. This book lends itself easily to a book discussion because of the structured opportunities for reflection and idea generation.

If you do decide to set up a book discussion group, here are some suggestions you might want to consider:

- Decide whether the group will follow the chronological sequence of the book or read selected sections.
- Set realistic meeting dates based on group members' availability. You may find, for example, that meeting once per month is a workable option.
- Choose a facilitator for each meeting. The facilitator kicks off the discussion, ensures that all members have their voices heard, and wraps up the discussion on time.
- Encourage all members to jot notes in response to the reflection questions, rather than relying on memory. Busy teachers can easily forget what they were thinking yesterday!
- Remember to honor everyone's thoughts and ideas. One of the key benefits of a book discussion is the variety of perspectives that are offered. New outlooks and solutions may appear when least expected!

Best Practices & Daily Practices at a Glance

It is common to hear teachers say "I haven't thought of that in years!" or "I used to do that, and I don't know why I stopped." Teachers are just so busy that good ideas often get lost in the shuffle—but the strategies in this book are ones that you are not going to want to forget! The Ideas at a Glance chart on page 12 is designed to help keep them in plain view and readily available. It lists the nine best practices and the four daily practice ideas for each. Make a copy and place it in your lesson-planning book or another visible location. Then, when you are stumped for an engaging activity to solidify your lesson, take a glance, make a choice, and launch your students on a learning adventure.

Ideas at a Glance

Best Practice	First Quarter Daily Practice Idea	Second Quarter Daily Practice Idea	Third Quarter Daily Practice Idea	Fourth Quarter Daily Practice Idea
Increasing Participation	Magic Prop Bag	Welsh Stomp	I'm In!	Pump It Up
Focusing Attention	Writer's Revision Tool	Vegetable Head	Purposeful Reading Tool	Secret Questions
Identifying Similarities & Differences	Concept Continuum	Scrambled Eggs	Bottle-Cap Sort	Metaphor Machine
Using Non-Linguistic Representations	Emoticons	5 Senses Graphic Organizer Puzzle	Director's Clapboard	SNAP Shot
Making Connections	Connection Puzzles	Idea Suitcases	Lighting Up the Brain	Brainy News
Determining Importance	Time Capsules	Forever Fortune Cookies	Bull's Eye	Position Mixers
Strengthening Memory	Spelling & Vocabulary Shapes	Spelling CD	Secret Code Books	Flashlight Tag
Summarizing	Summarization Man	Human Machines	Instant Messaging	Google Key Word Meter
Challenging Thinking	Passing Time	Mystery Box	Wow 'Em Challenges	Complete a Comic

First Quarter
First Quarter

BEST PRACTICE

Increasing Participation

Our brains are constantly scanning incoming sensory information. When the brain perceives any information as novel, norepinepherine is released, alerting the brain to the new input (Ratey, 2001). Focus on the new input is increased until it is processed by the brain. We ask, "Is this something that will sustain my interest?" If the answer is "no," we move on and continue to scan our environment.

If novelty is so successful in grabbing the brain's attention, then it is an important tool in every teacher's toolbox. Susan Jones, educator and author, writes, "To effectively lead students on the learning pathway, teachers must first grab attention. If none is paid, the subsequent milestones in planting memory will never be reached. No attention?—no activity. No activity?—no learning" (Jones, 2003).

Reflective Questions

- During the past week, what novel experiences did you encounter? How did you react to them?
- How do your students react to novelty?
- Which lessons or periods of the day present the greatest challenge for incorporating novelty?

_____

_____

_____

_____

_____

Idea for Daily Practice

Magic Prop Bag

As the school year progresses, it can be more and more challenging to hit upon fresh ways to engage student attention. You see the students every day, they see you every day, and it seems hard to make anything seem new. The Magic Prop Bag strategy provides a very simple approach that can be used frequently throughout the year without losing the sense of novelty. It also incorporates tactile opportunities that can help sustain the attention of fidgety students.

Materials

A pillowcase, fabric sack, or other opaque container

Props related to lesson

How To

1. Choose a container that has some visual appeal. It may be a brightly colored pillowcase, a sack of similar size that is made of interesting fabric, a hard case that latches, or a box covered in gift wrap.

2. Before students arrive, gather one or more props related to the day's lesson. For example, in a math lesson on determining area, the objects might include an envelope, a CD case, and an empty cracker box. Or you can choose objects as simple as the textbook and markers that students will use throughout the lesson. Place the objects in the Magic Prop Bag (or Magic Prop Box) and close the container so the props are not visible.

3. At the beginning of the lesson, bring out the Magic Prop Bag. Peek into the bag and begin to rummage around in it. Add some theatrics to heighten students' curiosity and attract their attention.

4. Explain to students that this is a magic bag and that different things appear in it every day.

5. Slowly pull out one of the props related to the lesson. Watch your students—all eyes will be on the bag! After removing the prop, engage students in discussion relevant to the lesson objectives.

Additional Ideas

- If one of the students is especially fidgety during the discussion, give that student the object to hold onto and display to the rest of the class.

- To make the Magic Prop Bag strategy more age appropriate for secondary students, you may wish to call it simply a Prop Bag.

- Begin the lesson by stating the learning objective for the day, and then ask students to guess what objects might be in the Magic Prop Bag. This will stimulate connections to prior knowledge.

Reflections

How did the students respond? What evidence do you have that the strategy was successful? Are there adaptations to the strategy that you might try in the future? Other thoughts?

BEST PRACTICE

Focusing Attention

As state-wide, standardized testing was becoming the norm around the country in the early 2000s, a group of researchers decided to undertake a thorough investigation of just what factors typically resulted in better student scores on standardized tests. The researchers looked for common factors that led all learners, from high to low achievers, to improve their test outcomes. The results surprised them—they found that student success hinged, in large part, on a set of 12 core skills, which they labeled the "hidden skills of academic literacy." Unfortunately, researchers have also found that these skills often go untaught in public schools.

One of the 12 skills that the researchers identified as essential to reflective, successful learning was the ability to evaluate one's own work in progress (Silver, Strong, and Perini; 2007). Some students will need your help in learning how to focus their attention and evaluate their work. It's imperative that you provide struggling students with simple strategies for doing this. If you can incorporate a tactile element at the same time, that's even better.

Reflective Questions

- What strategies do you use to reflectively evaluate your own work?
- In class, do you model the specific steps or strategies you use in evaluating your work samples?
- What other opportunities exist during the week to explicitly teach the skill of evaluating work in progress?

_____

_____

_____

_____

_____

Idea for Daily Practice

Writer's Revision Tool

> "The Writer's Revision Tool has really helped me. I would get a C in writing if I didn't have that tool."
> —Emma L.

With the advent of computer software programs that provide spell check and grammar correction, we have seen a decline in the emphasis on editing skills in the classroom. Yet most student writing in schools is done without the use of a computer. Students need to be able to spot gross spelling errors and to understand correct punctuation and other basic mechanics of writing. Good writers also need to be able to notice other facets of effective writing such as varied sentence length, interesting word choice, attention-getting starters, and the use of literary devices. The Writer's Revision Tool provides learners with a way to focus their editing and revising process on specific characteristics of effective writing. Through this focused reflection, each student will be able to make improvements that will lead to a solid piece of written work.

Materials

Reproducible #1

Cardstock

2 sheets of acetate in each of 4 colors (red, blue, green, and yellow)

Tape

How To

1. Choose four characteristics of good writing that are appropriate for the level of your students. Write each characteristic along one edge of the tool, on the blank line provided.

2. Make one copy of the reproducible, on cardstock, for every two students.

3. If desired, laminate each rectangle for greater durability.

4. Cut the acetate into 1-inch strips.

5. Working with one tool at a time, tape one strip of colored acetate to the back of each edge, allowing approximately two-thirds of the strip to clear the edge. Use each of the four colors on each tool, being careful to see that the colors and corresponding characteristics are the same on all the tools you make.

6. When students have completed a draft of a writing assignment, distribute the Writer's Revision Tools. Explain to students that it is important for them to perform a focused review of their work in order to make corrections for their final copy.

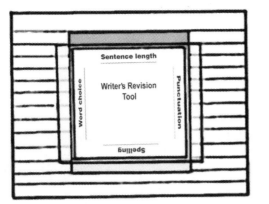

7. Model for students how to slide the Writer's Revision Tool down a page of writing, one line at a time, looking through the acetate for a specific characteristic. For example, if red corresponds to spelling errors, have students look at each line through the red acetate, searching for spelling errors. Direct students to stop and mark errors that need correction.

8. After scanning their papers for one characteristic, each student should turn her tool so that another color and characteristic are at the top, then repeat Step #7.

Additional Ideas

⚙ Create leveled Writer's Revision Tools using different characteristics. For example, one might have basic characteristics appropriate to the grade level, while another might have challenges for students who are ready for greater complexity (for example, these could include alliteration, metaphor, onomatopoeia, and dialogue).

⚙ The back side of the Writer's Revision Tool is blank, making it possible to use this as a focus tool in almost any subject. To adapt the tool for other parts of the curriculum, use a wet-erase marker, such as an overhead transparency pen, to write a focus point along each edge. For example, in math class the four focus points might be operational signs, decimal points, commas, and answers. In a history class, the four criteria might include location, date, event, and people.

Reflections

How did the students respond? What evidence do you have that the strategy was successful? Are there adaptations to the strategy that you might try in the future? Other thoughts?

_____

_____

_____

_____

_____

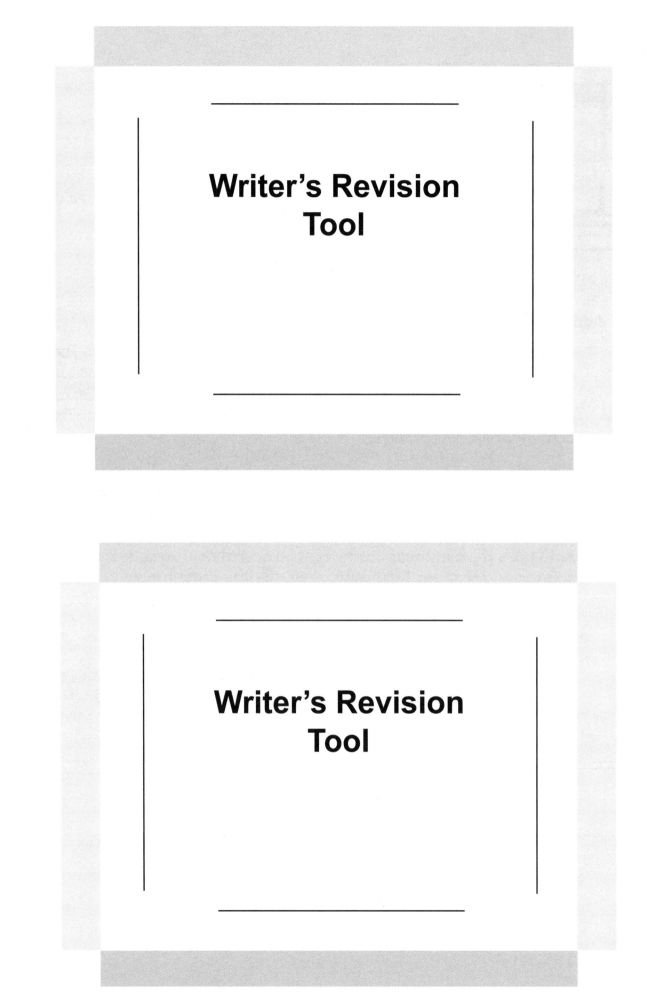

Writer's Revision
Tool

Writer's Revision
Tool

BEST PRACTICE

Identifying Similarities & Differences

Because you have limited face-to-face time with students, you know you must make every teaching moment powerful. Strategies that help students learn how to identify similarities and differences have been shown to enhance achievement by as much as 40 percentile points (Marzano, 1988). That's powerful!

The process of comparison can be applied to word study in many ways. Teachers often have students sort words by word families, vowel sounds, and parts of speech. But for students to truly understand the meaning of new vocabulary, it is critical that they have a deeper level of understanding. Deborah Knight (2006) suggests that there are five levels of word knowledge:

1. No knowledge
2. General sense of the word without being able to define it
3. Narrow, context-bound knowledge
4. Knowledge of the word, but without the ability to recall it readily for appropriate use
5. Rich, decontextualized knowledge of the word's meaning and relationship to other words

It is this fifth level to which we want our students to aspire. Here, students will be able to identify similarities and differences between words at a deep-meaning level. One way to get to that point, research tells us, is by using strategies for vocabulary instruction that incorporate associations with known synonyms (Gipe, 1978).

Reflective Questions

- What strategies do you use when acquiring a new word?
- What level of word knowledge do your students usually demonstrate?
- How much time do your students typically have to identify similarities and differences between each new word and previously acquired words?

Idea for Daily Practice

Concept Continuum

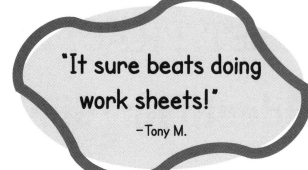

Some similarities and differences are fairly obvious—a square compared to a circle, a book compared to a movie—but others are more subtle. When they have explored the subtle differences between words or concepts, students are more likely to understand and remember the meaning of new vocabulary. Concept Continuum provides students with a collaborative group process for analyzing the similarities and differences in word meanings by sorting words along a continuum. This strategy also dispenses with predetermined, teacher-set "right answers," allowing for higher-level thinking among students.

Materials

Reproducible #2, 3, 4, or 5 OR your own set of concept vocabulary

How To

1. Choose one set of Concept Continuum vocabulary, based on student ability level, or substitute your own set of concept vocabulary words. Make one copy of the list per group.

2. Divide students into small groups. Give each group one set of Concept Continuum vocabulary words and direct them to cut the words apart.

3. Explain to students that they are to line up the words along an imaginary continuum. (If necessary, define *continuum*.) To determine the order, they will need to discuss the meanings of the words, including the similarities and differences, and come to an agreement about the order. Suggest that there is not necessarily a correct order in every case—but add that students should be prepared to justify their decisions.

4. Model with an example on the board or overhead projector. Engage students in a whole-group discussion about the similarities and differences in the words, and how that might play into the order in which they place the words. For example, if the words are *small, tiny, minute, mini, little, insignificant, microscopic,* and *modest,* the continuum might look like one of the following:

   • microscopic, insignificant, minute, tiny, mini, little, small, modest

   • microscopic, minute, insignificant, tiny, mini, small, little, modest

5. Wander around the classroom and check in with groups as they are developing their continuums.

6. When sufficient time has passed, ask groups to share their continuums. Discuss any differences as a class.

7. Promote strong curriculum associations for your students by generating Concept Continuum vocabulary for your own themes or units. Choose one representative word and use a thesaurus to find seven or more synonyms or related words.

Additional Ideas

✸ Increase the tactile aspect of this activity by writing the concept words onto Popsicle sticks and distributing those to students instead of handing out pieces of paper.

✸ Provide each group with some clothespins and a piece of rectangular poster board. Have them pin their words on their continuum in the order they've chosen. Ask them to hold up the poster board to show the class.

✸ Color code Concept Continuum vocabulary by subject area so that you or the students can grab and use them quickly.

✸ For younger students, try using just four or five words. Add words as students become more skilled at the activity.

✸ Print words on larger pieces of paper or on 4 x 6-inch index cards. Ask students to stand in front of the room, with each child holding one word, to show their continuum.

Reflections

How did the students respond? What evidence do you have that the strategy was successful? Are there adaptations to the strategy that you might try in the future? Other thoughts?

_____

_____

_____

_____

_____

happy	happy	happy
content	content	content
joyful	joyful	joyful
glad	glad	glad
delighted	delighted	delighted
pleased	pleased	pleased
cheerful	cheerful	cheerful
elated	elated	elated

freedom	freedom	freedom
liberty	liberty	liberty
autonomy	autonomy	autonomy
independence	independence	independence
choice	choice	choice
self-determination	self-determination	self-determination
free will	free will	free will
options	options	options

quantity	quantity	quantity
number	number	number
measure	measure	measure
extent	extent	extent
magnitude	magnitude	magnitude
amount	amount	amount
total	total	total
integer	integer	integer

process	process	process
method	method	method
procedure	procedure	procedure
development	development	development
technique	technique	technique
system	system	system
formula	formula	formula
modus operandi	modus operandi	modus operandi

BEST PRACTICE

Using Non-Linguistic Representations

While reading is often thought of as mainly a linguistic task, it involves many other cognitive processes as well. Through the use of imaging technology, researchers have discovered that reading activates areas in both the left and right hemispheres of the brain. Some educators believe that the act of reading can incorporate all of the brain's multiple intelligences (Armstrong, 2003). While many students succeed with the word-based approach used in schools, other students may be more successful with non-linguistic supports.

The question then becomes what supports might be most effective. In a study done at Emory University, researchers used magnetic resonance imaging (MRI) to measure emotional responses to words. The study found that when emotions were stimulated, activity increased in areas of the brain that form memories, causing learners to remember twice as many words with emotional connections as words with no such connections (Hamann, Ely, Gafton, and Kilts; 1999). Emotion is a powerful tool for enhancing memory!

Reflective Questions

- When reading for pleasure, what emotions do you experience?
- How frequently are your students encouraged to respond emotionally to what they are reading in fiction? In nonfiction?
- Some students struggle with expressing emotion. How can you support them?

Idea for Daily Practice

Emoticons

Emoticon is a fusion of the words emotion and icon. Emoticons are symbols used to convey emotional content. Found in documents as early as the mid-1800s, they came into popular use with the introduction of the smiley face in 1963. Emoticons are now a highly recognizable feature of e-mail, instant messages, text messages, ad campaigns, and most technology-enhanced communication. Because of their link to popular culture, these symbols are enticing to students of all ages. They also boost engagement of students who may need linguistic support. The visual images serve as strong comprehension and expression cues for all students.

Materials

Reproducible #6

Magnets or sticky tack

Restickable adhesive sticks

How To

1. Make one copy of the reproducible for each student, plus one for yourself.

2. Cut out one set of emoticons for your model. Attach a magnet or sticky tack to the back of each emoticon so that the symbols can be placed on the board.

3. Write the word *emoticon* on the board and ask students if they are familiar with the term. Choose a student to define the word and give examples.

4. Explain that emotional responses to reading are natural and that they aid readers in understanding and remembering content.

5. Display your emoticons on the board. Ask the students to describe the emotion that each symbol might represent; write the descriptive words next to the symbol. Then ask the students what color might best represent each emotion; color the paper symbols accordingly.

6. Distribute the reproducibles to students and have them color and cut out the symbols.

7. Apply a dab of restickable adhesive to the back of each emoticon. Have each student stick his symbols to the inside cover of his book or reading material.

8. Write the title of a reading selection on the board.

9. Begin a whole-group reading of that selection. After several paragraphs, stop and prompt the students to discuss relevant emotions. For example, when reading fiction, prompt with a question such as "How do you think the character is feeling

right now?" or "How do you feel about what just happened?" If the class is reading nonfiction, prompts might include "How do you feel about what you just learned?" or "How do you think the people who are affected by this might feel?" As students contribute, have them come up to the board and move the appropriate emoticon under the title.

10. Move from whole-group reading to individual reading. Direct students to use their own emoticons as they are reading to note passages that evoked emotions for them. Stop after an appropriate amount of time and ask students to share their emotional responses.

11. Suggest that students keep their emoticons in their current reading material so that they can use the emoticons whenever they do independent reading.

Additional Ideas

☀ Keep emoticons on the board or on a surface near your read-aloud area. During read-aloud times, stop occasionally and ask a student to choose an emoticon that best represents the emotion of the moment.

☀ Copy the emoticon reproducible onto a magnet sheet, available at office supply stores. Cut the individual icons apart and then apply the emoticon magnets to any magnetic surface; they will stick easily.

☀ Use emoticons during nonreading instructional activities as well. Emoticons might be helpful during lessons on conflict resolution, for example, or as part of discussions about controversial topics, classroom rules, or reflections on a learning experience.

☀ Some students struggle with identifying and expressing emotions, perhaps as a result of a specific learning disability or emotional difficulty or because they are still learning the English language. Consider a discussion with additional personnel, such as a school psychologist, speech/language pathologist, or ELL specialist to develop additional ideas for using emoticons with these students.

Reflections

How did the students respond? What evidence do you have that the strategy was successful? Are there adaptations to the strategy that you might try in the future? Other thoughts?

_____

_____

_____

_____

BEST PRACTICE

Making Connections

A psychological principle known as clozentropy suggests that when the mind is presented with incomplete information, it is motivated to fill in gaps (Marzano, 2007). This might explain why crossword puzzles, Sudoku games, and other activities that present "holes" to be filled are such popular ways to pass the time. You can take advantage of this natural inclination and increase student engagement by providing students with manufactured holes.

Another powerful way to increase engagement with new information is to provide students with opportunities to make personal connections. As students make connections between new information and previous knowledge or experience, they strengthen neuronal connections. In addition, motivation increases because students have the opportunity to talk and think about things that interest them.

Reflective Questions

- What "holes" do you come across in your life that you feel motivated to fill?
- How do you encourage students to make connections between new learning and their previous knowledge and experiences?
- In what curriculum area do you want to increase connections for students?

Idea for Daily Practice

Connection Puzzles

Puzzles have a game-like quality about them that engages student interest. Connection Puzzles use this to encourage students to make connections between new information and previous knowledge or experience. Students' desire to complete the class Connection Puzzle increases the likelihood that they will make the effort to think of a connection between prior knowledge and the new content. The puzzle also provides you with an easy way to track which students have made connections and which have not. You can then provide additional encouragement to students who need it.

Materials

1 magnet sheet for computer printers

Permanent marker

How To

1. Use a computer to design a small text box that says "We Made Connections." Print this in the middle of an 8 1/2 x 11-inch magnet sheet. (If you prefer, draw the box by hand with a permanent marker.)

2. With permanent marker, write each student's name on an area of the magnet sheet.

3. Cut the paper into puzzle pieces, so that each student's name is on its own piece. Leave the "We Made Connections" piece whole.

4. Place the "We Made Connections" piece on the board, in an area where it can be left throughout the week without being disturbed.

5. Draw a larger rectangle, slightly larger than 8 1/2 x 11 inches, positioning it so that the text box is in the center of the large rectangle. Your puzzle will take shape in the space around the text box.

6. Place each of the name pieces randomly on the board around the puzzle area.

7. Explain to students that throughout the week, if a student makes a connection between what she is learning and another piece of knowledge or experience, she will be allowed to connect her puzzle piece to the puzzle. The goal is to complete the puzzle by the end of the week (or unit, chapter, and so on).

8. As more and more name pieces are moved into the rectangle, it will become easier to connect them and to see the holes in the puzzle. Once you've identified students whose pieces are not yet connected, encourage them to think of connecting concepts, events, books, or examples from life outside of the classroom. Students whose pieces have already been attached should be encouraged to continue to make connections in their minds.

Additional Ideas

- Instead of using magnet sheets, buy blank cardboard jigsaw puzzles. (These are available from several online sources—just search on "blank cardboard jigsaw puzzles.") Purchase puzzles that have at least one piece for every member of the class. Write student names on the individual pieces and attach a small piece of magnet tape to the back of each piece. You may want to leave a few pieces blank in case new students move in during the year. Aside from that, fill any blank spaces with phrases such as "we made connections."

- If you do not have a magnetic surface in your classroom, obtain a blank cardboard jigsaw puzzle, write a student name on each puzzle piece, and place some sticky tack on the back of each piece.

- If you have several different classes throughout the day, obtain one puzzle for each class and have students write their names on the pieces. Attach the pieces to the inside of a file folder using sticky tack. Open the folder and tack it up on the board during the class period, and then replace it as classes change.

- Choose a specific type of connection that you would like students to make. For example, you might want students to attach their puzzle pieces only if they have made a text-to-text connection, or only if they have identified a connection between math and careers.

Reflections

How did the students respond? What evidence do you have that the strategy was successful? Are there adaptations to the strategy that you might try in the future? Other thoughts?

_____

_____

_____

_____

_____

BEST PRACTICE

Determining Importance

Determining importance is an essential stepping stone in the comprehension process. Appraising information and deciding to retain or discard it involves important, higher-level cognition. Overload comes quickly for students who do not know how to discard the excess information they take in daily. And in response to overload, many students simply shut down. These students need a wide variety of opportunities to practice the art and science of determining which ideas are important.

Opportunities that link outdoor learning with comprehension can strengthen student understanding and memory. Steven Wolk proposes several essentials that should be built into every school day; one of those is simply getting outside (Wolk, 2008). Fresh air, natural light, movement, and hands-on opportunities all enrich the learning experience when that experience takes place outdoors.

Reflective Questions

- Do you notice a difference in yourself when you're involved in indoor versus outdoor learning experiences? If so, what is that difference?
- What are some examples of situations that cause your students to struggle with determining important concepts?
- Given your school environment, what are some ways to incorporate outdoor learning experiences?

Idea for Daily Practice

Time Capsules

"If I could save time in a bottle, the first thing that I'd like to do is to save. . . ." These song lyrics by Jim Croce portray a natural human desire to capture important feelings and memories for posterity. Much of the time, it seems as if our brains act almost independently of us in determining which memories are the most important to save. But you can preempt that process. Through strategic planning, you can guide students in determining the most important knowledge about a topic to "save in a bottle." The Time Capsule strategy engages students in the selection of materials that represent the most important things to know about a topic. Students then bank this memory by burying the time capsule in the schoolyard (or hiding it somewhere in the building), to be uncovered at a later time.

Materials

A watertight plastic container

A shovel

How To

1. At the end of a unit of study, explain to students that they will be assembling a time capsule about the topic they have been studying. Show them the container that they will be filling, so they can get an idea of its size.

2. Elicit from students various ideas of what should be included in the time capsule to best represent their learning. Encourage students to discuss the pros and cons of each item until they are able to reach a consensus about which would be the best items.

3. Have students compose a letter to next year's class concerning what those students will uncover in the time capsule. This year's class can also generate clues or a map for finding the capsule. (If you prefer, this same class can uncover the time capsule later in the school year.)

4. Take the students outside to bury the time capsule. Allow each student a turn at digging up the patch of earth. Carefully cover the capsule and, if desired, place a marker of some kind to indicate where it is buried.

5. Next year, dig it up!

Additional Ideas

⚙ Divide the class into four groups and direct each group to put together their own time capsule.

⚙ Have each student write a letter to one of next year's students describing the contents of the time capsule and why each item is important.

* If digging a hole on school grounds is not possible, search for a place in the building that might lend itself to "burying" a time capsule (for example, a supply closet).

* Search the Internet for video footage of time capsules being uncovered and view them with the students.

* At the beginning of a unit, inform your students that when they complete the unit, they will be filling a time capsule with the best representations of their learning. Encourage them along the way to think of items that might best demonstrate their knowledge.

Reflections

How did the students respond? What evidence do you have that the strategy was successful? Are there adaptations to the strategy that you might try in the future? Other thoughts?

_____

_____

_____

_____

_____

BEST PRACTICE

Strengthening Memory

Memories are created and accessed through a variety of paths (Sprenger, 2005). The semantic path, dealing with words and language, is the one used most often in schools. Unfortunately, the semantic memory path can also be the most difficult for many of us to access. The episodic path, dealing with location and events, is easier for the brain to access. We usually find it less difficult to recall information when it is linked to a place, time, or event. This is why graphic organizers can be so helpful in retaining information. Graphic organizers link semantic information with a location on a page, thereby tapping into the most effective memory path.

Reflective Questions

- What helps you to remember things?
- Are there ways you can use location as a teaching and learning tool?
- How can you increase the use of graphic organizers throughout the week?

Idea for Daily Practice

Spelling & Vocabulary Shapes

> "I loved the Spelling Shapes because they helped me by creating a picture of the words in my head."
> –Tyler F.

Many students struggle with accurate spelling, and spelling programs that provide students with lists of words to memorize (using semantic memory) are not always helpful. Spelling & Vocabulary Shapes is a strategy that uses graphic organizers (targeting episodic memory) to increase retention of spelling, with an additional benefit of increasing the comprehension of word meaning.

Materials

Weekly spelling or vocabulary list

Black line figure (see suggestions below)

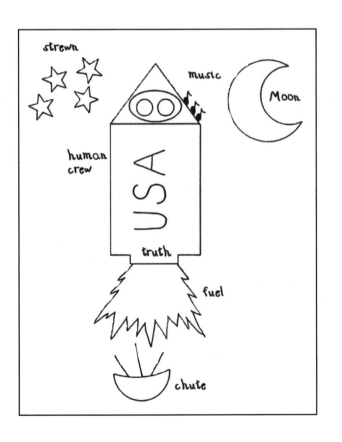

How To

1. Choose or draw a black line figure that has some associated meaning. Excellent choices include a stick person, a rocket ship, a baseball diamond, a bed, or a place setting at a dinner table.

2. Make one copy of the figure for each student and, if you like, one transparency to use in modeling.

3. In class, introduce the spelling or vocabulary list for the week. Explain to students that they will write each of the words on their handouts after the class discusses the meaning of the word.

4. Hand out the student copies of the figure. Place the transparency on the overhead or draw the figure on the board.

5. Read the first word on the list. Ask the students what it means to them. Discuss the correct meaning of the word and then ask students where it might make the most sense to write it on the figure. For example, if the figure is of a rocket ship and the word is *strewn,* a student might suggest that because stars are scattered or strewn across the sky, it makes sense to draw some stars and write the word *strewn* next to them.

6. Demonstrate on the transparency or board, and ask students to mark their copies accordingly.

7. Continue this process for each word on the list.

8. After the class completes the shape, direct each student to store her copy in a study folder. Encourage students to study for their spelling or vocabulary test by looking over the shapes, closing their eyes, and picturing the location and spelling of each word.

9. Immediately before students take their test, remind them to close their eyes and picture the shape if they have difficulty with a word.

Additional Ideas

☼ As students get more experience with *Spelling & Vocabulary Shapes*, direct individuals to place the words wherever they feel they make the most sense (rather than deciding as a group).

☼ Encourage older students to develop their own shapes after looking at the list of words.

☼ Use shapes to solidify the retention of any new vocabulary. Whenever introducing multiple vocabulary terms in a content unit, choose a simple shape and have students write the terms on the shape instead of as a list. For example, in a geometry unit with words such as *coordinate*, *congruent*, *slope*, and *symmetry*, have students draw a simple outline of a car and discuss meaningful places to add the words.

Reflections

How did the students respond? What evidence do you have that the strategy was successful? Are there adaptations to the strategy that you might try in the future? Other thoughts?

_____

_____

_____

_____

_____

BEST PRACTICE

Summarizing

All students think, but not all students think skillfully. Skillful thinking involves being reflective, analytical, evaluative, and creative. Skillful thinking comes easily to some, but needs to be modeled and explicitly taught to most. Instruction must also be followed by practice in context so that the thinking skills become ingrained for each student (Costa, 2008).

Summarization, the ability to capture the essence of a large piece of information in a small number of words, is one of the most important thinking skills for enhancing student achievement (Marzano, Pickering, and Pollock; 2001). We expect students to summarize their learning throughout their school day—as we ask questions of them during discussions, when we assign homework that directs them to explain a scientific process, when we ask them to write book reports, and when standardized tests require them to answer questions about text excerpts.

In order for students to be most successful with summarization, they need to be thinking this way even when they're not being explicitly asked to. Successful students are summarizing their teacher's lectures as they hear them. They write notes to themselves in the margins of books to capture the main ideas. They share with parents a summary of what they learned at school. But some students may struggle with summarizing because of its heavy reliance on language. Instructional strategies that incorporate symbolic representations or movement broaden the opportunities for all students to be successful.

Reflective Questions

- During what day-to-day, nonschool activities do you engage in summarizing?
- How skilled are your students at summarizing? What are their strengths? Weaknesses?
- Because summarizing can be seen as an intangible, "in-your-head" thinking process, how can you make it more concrete and active for your students?

Idea for Daily Practice

Summarization Man

The Summarization Man strategy is a multimodality approach to making the thinking skill of summarizing more concrete and memorable for students. Summarization Man provides a visual representation of the thinking process, pairs it with kinesthetic movements to strengthen retention, and adds an auditory chant to build automaticity. The strategy is flexible enough that it can be used during group discussions or with book reports, expository writing, research projects, or reviewing at home for a test.

Materials

Reproducible #7

How To

1. Make one copy of the reproducible for each student, plus one transparency, if you like, for modeling purposes.

2. Provide each student with a copy of the Summarization Man. Place the transparency on the overhead projector or draw a Summarization Man on the board.

3. Explain that the Summarization Man will help everyone to remember four major components of an effective summarization. Identify the four components as:

   - Head: the main idea
   - Heart: the feeling or emotion associated with the main idea
   - Hand: one key fact, detail, event, or characteristic
   - Hand: one key fact, detail, event, or characteristic

4. Provide additional explanation as necessary.

5. Lead students in a choral chant of "Head, heart, hand, and hand make a Summarization Man." Repeat the chant three times.

6. Demonstrate the physical movements that correspond to the parts of the chant:
   - Head: both hands on the top of the head
   - Heart: both hands over the heart
   - Hand: hold one hand out to the side
   - Hand: hold the other hand out to the side

7. Have students say the chant and practice the movements three times.

8. Use the Summarization Man to summarize a story, video, or lesson that students are familiar with. Model the strategy for students by writing the summarization ideas on the transparency in each of the four component areas.

9. Provide the students with material to be summarized. The material might be a short story, a recent lesson, or a research project they have just completed. Direct them to use the Summarization Man reproducible to plan their summary, just as you have modeled.

10. Select several students and ask each to share her summary in the front of the class, using the appropriate movements as she describes the four components.

Additional Ideas

☀ Use the *Summarization Man* at various times throughout the week to summarize a lesson or story that the class has just read. Instead of providing each student with a handout, draw the *Summarization Man* on the board or chart.

☀ Older students can use *Summarization Man* as a part of their note-taking process. At the end of a week or unit of instruction, direct students to draw a *Summarization Man* next to their notes and use the figure to capture the main ideas of the section.

☀ Use the *Summarization Man* during a read-aloud that takes place over several days. *Summarize* at the end of the first session. At the beginning of the next session, show students a blank *Summarization Man* and ask students to share what they recall.

Reflections

How did the students respond? What evidence do you have that the strategy was successful? Are there adaptations to the strategy that you might try in the future? Other thoughts?

Head, heart, hand, and hand make a Summarization Man.

BEST PRACTICE

Challenging Thinking

"In order to teach well, one must be able to question well (Brualdi, 1998)." Teachers are reported to spend as much as 80% of their talk time with students asking questions. But in order for questions to be helpful to student learning, they should be chosen with specific purposes in mind. Low-level, concrete questions are most common in classrooms, and those are necessary for understanding and remembering basic information. However, higher-level questions are necessary to make learners think, pause, reflect, and explore (Conklin and Frei, 2007). The effective classroom teacher is careful to ask students both types of questions throughout the day.

Reflective Questions

- How much time do you personally spend reflecting on abstract, creative, "what if" questions?
- What percentage of the questions you ask students call for higher-level thinking?
- What type of structure can you build into your week that will ensure that you ask more high-level questions of your students?

Idea for Daily Practice

Passing Time

The Passing Time strategy takes advantage of the minutes that students spend passing from your class to the next activity by providing them with a thought-provoking question just before they step out the door. The questions are generic enough so that they can be applied to almost any lesson content. Therefore, you can prepare them in advance and use them over the course of several weeks—having a built-in structure for questioning without any day-to-day preparation.

Materials

Reproducible #8

Reproducible #9

Sticky tack or tape

How To

1. Make several copies of Reproducible #8. Cut the clocks apart (keeping the blank back attached to each clock face) and laminate them.

2. Make one copy of any page of Reproducible #9. Cut apart the individual questions.

3. Fold the clock cutouts in half, so that the clock face is on the front of each.

4. Stick a question inside each clock, adhering it to the back circle.

5. Place the clocks around the door jamb so that they are visible as students are getting ready to leave the classroom.

6. As everyone is lining up to change classes, select a student near the front of the line to choose a clock, open it up, and read the question inside it.

7. Encourage the students to "pass the time" in the hallway thinking about the answer to the question. For example, let's say the lesson is about acute and obtuse angles, and the question is, "If this lesson were a flavor of ice cream, what would it be? Would it be chunky or creamy? Why?" Students might generate answers such as:

    *   "It would be chocolate chunk, because when chocolate breaks, it sometimes has a sharp angle."

    *   "It would have a tart taste, like lime, because the flavor is sharper like the points of an angle."

    *   "Acute ice cream would be nonfat, and obtuse would be made with whole milk and very creamy."

    *   "Obtuse ice cream would be a mix of all kinds of chunky things, because obtuse angles are big enough to include variety."

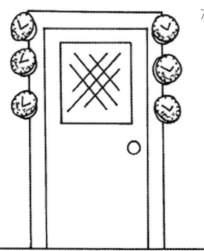

8. When students return to class, remind them of the question and ask them what answers they thought of as they passed through the hallways.

9. Change the questions every few weeks so that students will have new challenges to explore.

Additional Ideas

⚙ Encourage students to think up new questions that can be put inside the clocks. Remind them that the questions should be higher level and generic enough to fit any lessons. Show them several questions as models.

⚙ Consider other times during the week when the Passing Time strategy might be appropriate. Perhaps there are moments when students are waiting for the Pledge, finished with a test, or packing their materials to go home, when they could be occupying their brains with an interesting question.

⚙ Place students into mixed-ability groups. Choose a question and ask students to consider their answer silently. Have individuals share their answer with their group members. Call on a few students to share their answers with the whole class.

Reflections

How did the students respond? What evidence do you have that the strategy was successful? Are there adaptations to the strategy that you might try in the future? Other thoughts?

_____

_____

_____

_____

_____

If you were to have a bumper sticker on your car about this concept, what would it say?

If this concept were a flavor of ice cream, what would it be? Would it be chunky or creamy? Why?

If you could go back home and change clothes to fit this lesson, what would you wear and why?

If this concept were a song, what genre of music would it be and what title would you give it?

If this concept were a store in the mall, what would it be called and what would you buy there?

If you were to find something on eBay related to this lesson, what would it be and how much would it auction for?

If you were creating a Web page for this concept, what would it look like?

If you were a ballroom dancer, how would you express this concept?

If you were to do a Google search about this lesson, what 3 keywords would you enter for your search?

If you were to develop a product related to this lesson, what would it be?

If you were to design a reality TV show based on this lesson, what would it be called and what would it be about?

If you were to put this concept into an illustration, picture, or graphic design, what would it look like?

If you were a politician, how would you campaign on this issue?

If this lesson were written up in a tabloid, what would the headline be?

If this content were to be discussed on a TV talk show, which show would it be best suited to and why?

If you were to design a video or computer game for this lesson, what would the objective be?

If you saw a commercial on TV about this concept, what would it look like?

If you were in charge and could change some part of this information, what would you change?

Where would you travel to find this lesson concept in action?

If this lesson were highlighted on the evening news, what would be the headline?

How could you change this concept to illustrate the opposite effect?

When have you used this information outside of class?

Given a million dollars, how would you use this information to benefit society?

If this lesson were a sport, what would it be called and how would it be played?

If this lesson were represented by a cartoon character, who would it be and why?

How would you text message this lesson to someone?

If this lesson were turned into a party, what would the theme and decorations be?

How would life be different if this concept didn't exist?

If you were to watch this lesson on TV, what channel would it be on and why?

How might this lesson concept be related to an assembly line?

If this topic were a garden, what would you grow?

If this concept were a food, what would it be? Why?

If you were a journalist, what facts from this lesson would you include in your newspaper article?

If this concept were a mode of transportation, what type would it be and where would it take you? Why?

If this topic were a menu, what would be included?

What career would this lesson help you in and why?

If school were an amusement park, what kind of ride would this lesson be? Why?

If this concept were a pet, what would it need to grow and be healthy?

If this lesson were represented in an art gallery, what would the work of art look like?

What screen name would you choose to convey that you really love this topic?

If you had to create a CD about this lesson, what would the album and song titles be?

If this topic were a movie, how long would it be and what would it be rated?

If you were teaching this lesson to a pet, how would you teach it?

If you were playing Monopoly, what property would this lesson represent and why?

If this lesson were related to a shape, what would the shape be and why?

What cartoon character would benefit most from this lesson and why?

What type of weather would be most closely related to this lesson? Why?

What two or three foods would you choose to go with this lesson and why?

If you could place something from this lesson in a time capsule, what would it be and why?

What style of shoe most represents what you just learned? Why?

If this concept were a street, where would it begin and end? What streets would branch off from it?

If you were to create a ring tone that best describes this lesson, what would it sound like?

If this lesson were a vehicle, what would it be? Would it be fast or slow?

If someone from a different country were studying this lesson, how might their perception be different?

If you were to design a superhero to go with this lesson, what would his or her super powers be?

What clues would you give so someone could guess what this lesson was about?

If this lesson had been taught to a pioneer, how might it have changed history?

If van Gogh (or another artist) had painted this lesson, what would it have looked like?

Which character from a book or TV show would need to know this lesson? Why?

If this lesson had a personality, what character traits would it have? Why?

If you were standing in the middle of a painting of this lesson, what sounds would you hear?

If this lesson were in a Super Wal-Mart, what department would it be in? Why?

What season of the year would best represent this concept? Why?

What famous person would be the best spokesperson for this concept? Why? What would that person say?

If a famous person could teach this lesson to you, who would you choose? Why would they be good at it?

If you were captured by aliens, how would you use this information to help you escape?

If you could teach this lesson to someone in history, who would it be and why?

If this lesson were part of *Jeopardy,* what would the categories be called?

If you developed a new country, would you bring this concept with you? Why or why not?

Design a postcard in your mind about this lesson. What would it look like? Who would you send it to?

If you didn't know the language the teacher was speaking, what would you think this lesson was about and why?

If this concept were a holiday, what would it be called and how would you celebrate it?

If your favorite musician were to write a song about this lesson, what would the first line of the lyrics say?

How would you explain the importance of this lesson to the President of the United States?

If you designed a T-shirt about this lesson, when and where would you wear it?

If you were an alien from another planet, what conclusions might you draw about humans from observing this lesson?

If this lesson had a machine representing it, what purpose would the machine have? What type of fuel would it use?

If this lesson were a news article, what picture would go with it and why? What would the caption say?

If you could create a toy to describe this lesson, what would it look like? What age group would it be for? How would you market it?

What concrete model might you build to display the concepts of this lesson? What materials would you use?

Do you think your grandparents were taught this idea in school? If so, would it have been taught the same way?

You are a baker. What type of cake or pastry would you design that symbolizes this lesson?

If you were putting this lesson on your i-Pod, what playlist would it go under? Why?

If the principal were to walk in right now, what 5 words would you use to explain to him or her what you were learning about?

If you had "show and tell" about this lesson, what would you bring in? Why?

What kind of an award might this lesson win? Why?

If you were to dream about this concept, what would you see?

Second Quarter

BEST PRACTICE

Increasing Participation

Learning experiences that are associated with positive emotions cause information to move into the brain's long-term memory system more easily (Willis, 2007). Teachers who want to improve student retention can use positive emotions to do so. But students need to access their memories as well. Researchers tell us that when negative emotions are paramount, it becomes more difficult to access the long-term memory system. Students who are stressed, fearful, anxious, or embarrassed have a more difficult time retaining the specific information they are supposed to be learning. A classroom culture that promotes positive relationships, helpful feedback, and celebrations of success will lead to greater learning than one that does not (Gregory and Kuzmich, 2005).

Studies also show that movement and exercise can cause an increase in students' rate of learning (Ratey, 2008). After experiencing movement, the brain is primed for quicker action. In classrooms this can translate into more productive learning time.

Reflective Questions

- How do you respond to positive feedback? How does it affect your memory?
- How many times in the last week did you celebrate a student's success?
- What are the best ways to provide positive feedback so that it can positively affect the learning climate of the classroom?

Idea for Daily Practice

Welsh Stomp

Simple celebrations are a type of encouragement that works well for the busy teacher. The Welsh Stomp is a celebration of student success that can be used on the spot, with no extra work on the teacher's part. Not only does it provide positive feedback to the student receiving the encouragement, but it also improves the attitudes of the students who are providing the Welsh Stomp. As an added bonus, the Welsh Stomp increases blood flow throughout the body (including the brain), thereby increasing alertness. For students who have lots of extra energy, the Welsh Stomp is a great energy outlet!

Materials

None!

How To

1. Select a time during the week when students might be presenting a project, reading a piece of writing aloud, or providing some other demonstration of learning that will lend itself well to positive group feedback.

2. Remind students that different cultures often have ways of communicating that are different from the ways we communicate in the United States. Explain that in Wales, audience members may show their gratitude for an excellent performance by stomping their feet on the floor rather than giving a standing ovation.

3. Announce that the class will be using the Welsh Stomp to help students celebrate their learning successes. Provide students with clear directions on the use of the Welsh Stomp—they will stomp their feet on the ground rapidly for three seconds and then be still.

4. Model for the students, and then give them a chance to practice.

5. After a student has finished a presentation of his work, provide the student with specific positive feedback on his work. Then ask the students to give him a Welsh Stomp!

Additional Ideas

* Collaborate with students to choose their own name for the stomp. They might choose to name it after the school, the town, or the school mascot.

* Students may want to explore ways that other cultures provide special recognitions—their equivalents of the standing ovation.

* Students might develop specific rhythmic stomps for specific purposes. For example, the "Wonderful Writing" stomp might be "slow, slow, fast, fast, fast."

Reflections

How did the students respond? What evidence do you have that the strategy was successful? Are there adaptations to the strategy that you might try in the future? Other thoughts?

_____

_____

_____

_____

_____

BEST PRACTICE

Focusing Attention

A veteran teacher once said, "My students are always paying attention. Now, if I can just get them to pay attention to the things I want them to pay attention to!" The brain is an active, always-on-the-lookout control center for the body. It's constantly attending to something. The goal for teachers and students is to guide that attention so that it is focused on important stimuli and can be sustained for an adequate period of time to accomplish the learning objective (Andreasen, 2001).

Students with diagnosed attention difficulties have an extra hard time focusing and sustaining attention on the one thing that their teacher has asked of them. Situations in which the input is primarily auditory seem to pose an additional challenge for many of these students, who often do better with multimodality input. As a result, when you need them to be actively listening—during lectures and read alouds, or when you're giving verbal directions, for example—their attention often wanders.

Yet literacy experts confirm what good teachers know: "active listening is especially important in the process of inquiry" and other high-level cognitive processes (Fountas and Pinnell, 2001). As Mel Levine, a professor of pediatrics, states, "A vibrant mind vibrates. While reading or listening, it engages in active dialogue, mentally jousting with the author or speaker (2007)." Active listeners are usually more efficient, productive, and successful students than passive listeners.

The good news is that research has shown that attention can be improved through targeted instruction and well-designed lesson activities. Incorporating visual, tactile, and kinesthetic opportunities can help all students improve their concentration and focus their attention.

Reflective Questions

- If you are listening to someone lecture or read aloud, what strategies do you employ to keep engaged?
- What evidence do you have that all of your students are paying attention during read-aloud times?
- What strategies have you taught your students to use during read-aloud times in fiction? Nonfiction?

_____

_____

_____

_____

Idea for Daily Practice

Vegetable Head

Many teachers and students find read-aloud time to be a favorite part of the day; students at almost every grade level usually welcome the opportunity to sit comfortably and listen to a compelling story. Observations of students during a read-aloud session usually yield pictures of students with their eyes on the teacher or with anticipation on their faces. But observations also yield questions about some students who don't seem to be demonstrating attentive behavior or who are clearly off-task. The Vegetable Head strategy, based on a familiar toy, motivates all students to be active listeners. It also provides tangible evidence that students are paying attention.

Materials

Reproducible #10

Black marker

1 sheet of poster board

Sticky tack

How To

1. Make one copy of the reproducible pages; cut the pieces apart and laminate them.

2. Use a black marker to draw a large oval in the center of the poster board, filling two-thirds of the space. Label the poster "Vegetable Head."

3. Place sticky tack on the poster in appropriate locations for two eyes, two ears, a nose, a mouth, some hair, and (just below the head) two hands.

4. Gather your students into a group for a read-aloud session. Begin by asking them if they are familiar with the popular Mr. Potato Head toy. Point out that the head of that toy is created by adding body parts to make something silly. Explain that they will do something similar with the Vegetable Head poster.

5. Show students the laminated body parts. Explain that writers use the various senses in their writing to capture a reader's attention with detailed descriptions. When students are participating in a read-aloud time, they should be listening for specific descriptions that the author used to engage the reader. If they notice one, they can choose a related body part and attach it to the poster. For example, if the description provides a vivid visual image, then the student who notices this can choose an eye to attach to the head. If the author describes a smell, the first student to notice can choose a nose to attach to the poster.

6. Continue reviewing all of the body parts with the students. When presenting the hair styles, ask students what they think these might represent. For example, perhaps they are for descriptions that make your hair stand on end; are surprising, emotional, or confusing; or give the perfect finishing touch. Have the students decide with you how best to use these parts.

7. Begin reading. As you come across a passage that is very descriptive, add vocal emphasis so that students recognize the sense being used. Many students will be raising their hands to participate. Choose a student to identify the descriptive element and the sense associated with it. Allow the student to choose any of the related body parts and attach it to the poster. Continue reading. (If students notice multiple examples of a specific sense, you may want to discuss the example and leave the original body part for this lesson or allow students to switch out the body part.)

8. At the end of the read-aloud session, ask your students to reflect on the author's writing style by looking at the head that has been created. What senses did the author use in his writing?

Additional Ideas

✿ Create individual Vegetable Heads using file folders and smaller body parts. (Use a copier or scanner to reduce the body parts to the desired size.) Provide one to each student during read-aloud times so that everyone can individually track the descriptions being used.

✿ Encourage students to use Vegetable Head when reviewing their own writing. When a student is finished with a writing assignment, direct her to draw a head on a piece of paper and then add eyes, ears, and so on for each sense she used in her work.

Reflections

How did the students respond? What evidence do you have that the strategy was successful? Are there adaptations to the strategy that you might try in the future? Other thoughts?

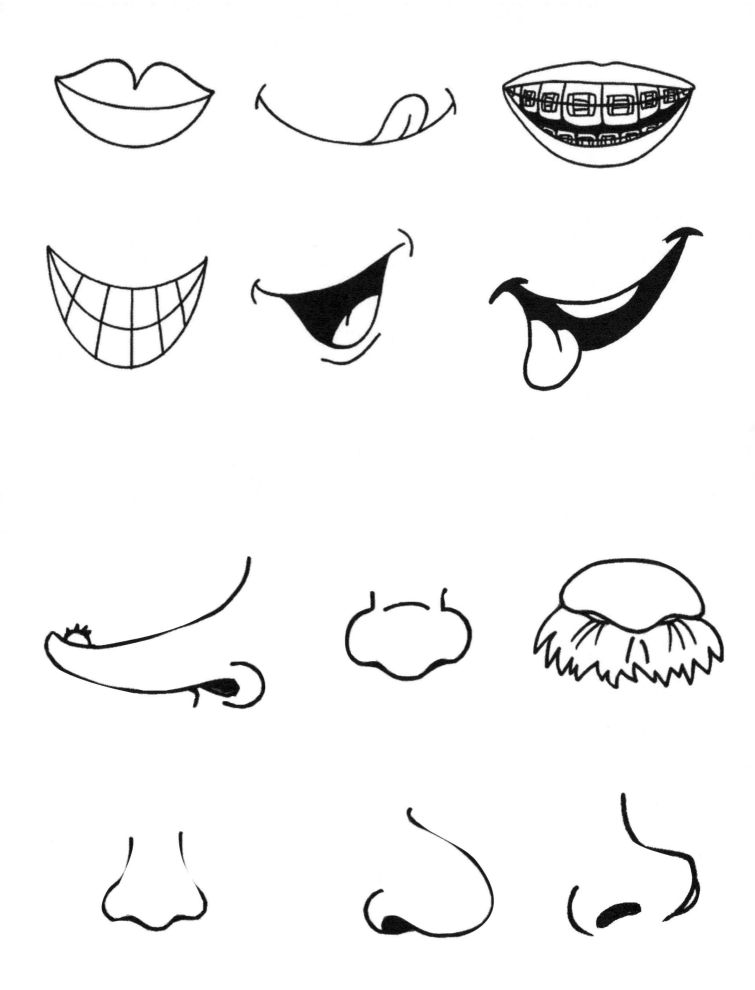

BEST PRACTICE

Identifying Similarities & Differences

We humans frequently compare items to find their similarities and differences. As Silver, Strong, and Perini state, "Humans love putting things in pairs—pass us a fork and we'll look for a knife; show us a setting sun and we'll try to find the rising moon (2007, p. 74)." The ability to notice pairs and sets generates numerous cognitive benefits—increasing memory, improving understanding, and generating creative new ideas. Comparative thinking is considered by some experts to be fundamental to learning (Garner, 2007).

A common practice in schools is to provide students with two or more categories and have them sort items or concepts into those categories. Teachers often jump in and point out features that students can use to make decisions. But current thinking in education suggests that students need to develop comparative thinking skills by recognizing the patterns for themselves, rather than relying on others to point them out. A more appropriate role for teachers is to provide opportunities for students to reflect and to recognize similarities and differences throughout their learning experience.

You can also strengthen student learning by adding physical movement to the process of identifying similarities and differences. Rather than just talking students through a complex cognitive skill, you can incorporate simple movement to increase the potential for learning. Every time we move our bodies, our brains release acetylcholine. This neurotransmitter stimulates the brain and yields new synaptic growth. The *neural pathways* become stronger (Jones, 2003)!

Reflective Questions

- What strategies do you use to sort pieces of information?
- What methods have you used to teach students to identify similarities and differences?
- How might you make those methods more physically interactive?

Idea for Daily Practice

Scrambled Eggs

Creative thought and comprehension are enhanced when students are out of their seats and fully engaged in enjoyable activities. Two-part plastic eggs ("Easter eggs") are a wonderful medium for accomplishing this. Available in a variety of bright colors, plastic eggs are usually associated with surprises, fun, and a boost of adrenaline. Paired with empty egg cartons, the eggs are ideally suited for sorting by similarities or differences. Top that off with the fact that you can write on the eggs with wet-erase markers, and you have a very versatile instructional strategy!

Materials

50–100 two-part plastic eggs ("Easter eggs") in a variety of colors

Wet-erase marker (also referred to as a transparency marker)

1/2 egg carton for every four students

How To

1. Before class, remove the top from each egg carton.

2. On the top of each egg write the name of a common object found in the home or at school. Use the ideas in the box (see next page) or generate your own.

3. Place the eggs in a bag or other large container.

4. Move the desks so that there is a large open-floor space available.

5. Divide the students into groups of four. Ask students to form one large circle on the floor, with group members seated next to each other.

6. Give each group an empty "six-pack" egg carton.

7. Explain to students that you will be pouring plastic eggs onto the floor. Show students a sample egg and explain that you've written a noun on the top of each one. Each group is to work together to find six of the Scrambled Eggs that have something in common. They should then place those eggs in their egg carton. (Remind students of the type of behavior you expect as they begin to scramble for their eggs.)

8. Pour the eggs onto the floor and step back to observe and direct.

9. When each group has filled their egg carton, call on students to explain the unifying characteristic of their eggs. For example, one group might have chosen "things that contain something" and have eggs labeled "journal," "pan," "book," "pillow," "balloon," and "wallet."

10. When everyone is finished, scramble the eggs again and direct students to find new similarities.

11. At the end of the lesson, ask student volunteers to rinse the writing off the eggs in the sink and pat them dry with a towel.

Additional Ideas

❋ Use concepts from your curriculum for a more focused sorting activity. For example, each egg used in a science unit might be labeled with the name of an animal.

❋ Because the eggs have tops and bottoms that separate, students can also use them to mix and match a variety of concepts. Rather than creating sets, students might pair prefixes with root words, nouns with verbs, states with capitals, numbers with their square roots, characters with traits, or words with synonyms or antonyms.

❋ Write student names on the tops of eggs and use the cartons to establish groups for a cooperative learning activity.

❋ In each egg deposit a small slip of paper that asks a question or provides a writing topic. Scramble the eggs and have each student pick one. Or hide the eggs around the classroom and have students go on an egg hunt!

Possibilities for Egg Labels

apple	box	computer	guitar	oven	radio	stapler
artwork	brush	crayons	hammer	pan	rocks	stool
baby	calculator	desk	ice	pants	rope	table
backpack	candle	door	journal	paper	rug	tape
bag	car	dresser	lamp	pen	ruler	teddy bear
ball	cards	envelope	magnet	pencil	scissors	television
balloon	carpet	flowers	mailbox	phone	screen	tissue
bed	cat	folder	map	photo	shampoo	towel
bell	cereal	fork	marker	piano	sheets	trashcan
bike	chair	games	milk	pillow	shoes	vase
blanket	chart	globe	mirror	plants	slippers	wallet
blocks	clay	glue	money	plate	soap	water
board	clock	grass	movie	popcorn	socks	whistle
book	coat	grill	newspaper	purse	sponge	window

✿ If plastic eggs aren't available, provide each group with a work sheet containing clip art of an egg carton. Write your words on egg-shaped pieces of colored paper, and have students glue them onto their egg cartons.

Reflections

How did the students respond? What evidence do you have that the strategy was successful? Are there adaptations to the strategy that you might try in the future? Other thoughts?

_____

_____

_____

_____

_____

BEST PRACTICE

Using Non-Linguistic Representations

"Words, words, words! Can't we ever do anything but words?" This lament from a struggling student represents the way many learners feel in school. Classrooms are filled with semantic instruction—but classrooms are also filled with students who are not strong linguistically. Graphic organizers offer a way for struggling students to succeed by learning semantic information through visual representations, an approach that can be more accessible to them.

Graphic organizers provide not only a visual stimulus, but also a way for students to link semantic information to a specific place on a piece of paper. This has a much stronger impact than just viewing those words in a paragraph or list. The combination of these two advantages makes graphic organizers one of the most effective instructional strategies that teachers have at their disposal (Marzano, Pickering, and Pollock; 2001).

But can we make this strategy even stronger? The typical approach to graphic organizers incorporates verbal and auditory information. By adding a tactile component, it is possible to grab and sustain the attention of students who need movement. Boys, in particular, often have so much energy that it can become a distraction if not channeled appropriately. Some educators believe that the reading and writing gender gap is a mismatch between the natural, active learning styles common to boys and the traditional visual and auditory instructional methods of schools (Gurian and Stevens, 2005).

Reflective Questions

- In what ways do you use graphic representations to help yourself learn or remember something in your life outside of school?
- Which of your students exhibit extra energy during reading and writing activities?
- How do you view and respond to energy-releasing behaviors such as pencil tapping, foot wiggling, chair tipping, and fidgeting?

Idea for Daily Practice

5 Senses Graphic Organizer Puzzle

"This helped a lot with planning because I struggle getting plans from my head to paper."
–Avid N.

Descriptive writing is enhanced when the writer provides details about sights, sounds, and smells—details our senses would provide us if we were actually experiencing the situation rather than reading about it. Even when students plan their writing with graphic organizers, they often concentrate on the organization of the main ideas and still ignore the value of descriptive detail. The 5 Senses Graphic Organizer Puzzle provides a structure that encourages students to build rich detail into their writing. The "puzzle pieces" extend the tactile input the student receives during the writing process, and the visual representations of the senses strengthen concept retention.

Materials

Reproducible #11

1 wet-erase marker per student

1 file folder per student

Sticky tack or tape for each student

How To

1. Make one copy of the reproducible pages per student. Laminate each copy.

2. Hand out the laminated copies. Have students cut out the 5 Senses puzzle pieces and place a small piece of sticky tack on the back of each.

3. Using the file folder as an organizing surface, demonstrate how the puzzle pieces can be arranged in multiple ways. For example, a circle might be placed in the middle, with three ovals around it and some of the five senses pieces distributed underneath the ovals. A second example might have a rectangle at the top with an oval underneath and a sense piece underneath it.

4. Explain to students that the Graphic Organizer Puzzles allow them to plan their writing in a way that is familiar to them, but that also allows them to move pieces into sequence as they develop their ideas. The 5 Senses pieces will remind them that they need to use the senses in their descriptions.

5. Show students how to write on the pieces with a wet-erase marker. Have each student adhere the puzzle pieces to an open file folder.

6. Provide students with time to plan a descriptive piece of writing. Wander the room and assist students in choosing the puzzle pieces that seem most appropriate for their content. Encourage them to write words in each of the shapes that capture their ideas succinctly. When time is up, direct students to save their ideas by closing the file folders and storing them in their desks or backpacks.

Additional Ideas

⚙ Encourage students to transfer this strategy to paper and pencil by drawing the 5 Senses visual representations into their writing plans. Using this technique on standardized assessments can dramatically increase the quality of descriptive writing a student produces.

⚙ Develop shapes that are specifically related to your content. For example, in a history lesson the shapes might include a globe (for location), a stick figure (for key people), a clock (for date or period of time), a starburst (for an event), and arrows (for cause and effect). When asking students to write in response to a question about history content, direct them to start by planning with the puzzle pieces.

⚙ Enlarge each of the pieces from the 5 Senses puzzle for use on a chart pad during whole-group lessons. Ask for volunteers to come up to the chart and record ideas on the puzzle pieces.

⚙ Use Graphic Organizer Puzzles during discussions to reinforce learning with visual and tactile cues. For example, during review of a specific chapter the class has read, individual students might complete puzzle pieces that represent the characters, events, setting, and action and attach them to the board.

Reflections

How did the students respond? What evidence do you have that the strategy was successful? Are there adaptations to the strategy that you might try in the future? Other thoughts?

_____

_____

_____

_____

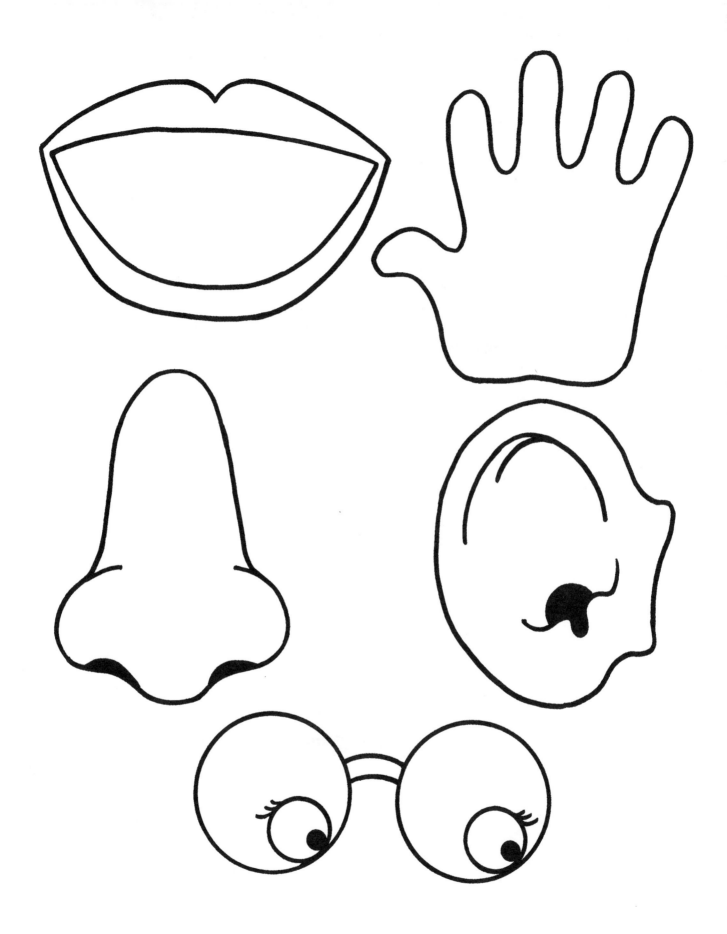

BEST PRACTICE

Making Connections

Researchers estimate that by the age of four, the typical child living in poverty may have been exposed to 30 million fewer words than a peer from a high-income family (Risley and Hart, 2003). This is a problem because vocabulary exposure is key to future language-arts success. For that reason, it is vitally important that you work to accelerate the vocabulary acquisition of any student who is behind in that area.

Most word learning is incremental. Students typically begin by learning a basic meaning and then develop deeper understandings through multiple exposures in different contexts (Scott and Nagy, 2000). In fact, research shows instruction that relies on definitions alone is not likely to increase comprehension (Baumann, Kame'enui, and Ash; 2003). Instead, children need to understand how a word may be generalized to apply in alternative contexts. Students who experience multiple exposures to a word, in a myriad of contexts, understand the word at a deeper level than those who learn the word in a single context (Hirsch, 2003). When the student makes a variety of connections, this strengthens the neural pathways and leads to better retention.

Reflective Questions

- After you have learned a new skill, what strategies do you use to try to generalize it and apply it to another context?

- What motivates some students to try to use new words in alternative contexts?

- How can you accelerate your students' exposure to new words in rich, meaningful contexts?

Idea for Daily Practice

Idea Suitcases

> "Idea suitcases help to plant seeds in my brain garden."
> —Perlina M.

Many students will be familiar with game shows in which contestants can choose to open one of several cases, doors, or curtains and uncover the prize hidden inside. Building on their familiarity with these game shows, the Idea Suitcases will generate enthusiastic interest as students wonder what each case holds. To strengthen comprehension of new vocabulary and assist in generalization, you can "fill" Idea Suitcases with labels representing "valuable vacation trips"—places students can go and use their new words.

Materials

Reproducible #12

Dry- or wet-erase marker

Sticky tack or Velcro

How To

1. Make 10 copies of the reproducible. Number the suitcases from one through 20.
2. Laminate the suitcases and cut them apart.
3. Place a small dot of sticky tack or Velcro on the handle of each suitcase.
4. Using a dry- or wet-erase marker, write the name of a location inside each suitcase.
5. Fold each suitcase in half. Crease the fold well so that the cases don't pop open!
6. Hang the suitcases on a wall or bulletin board where students can access them.
7. When introducing a new vocabulary word to students, share the definition of the word and discuss the meaning. Explain to students that it is important to know how to use words in settings other than school.

Possible "Vacation Destinations" for Suitcases

- a movie theater
- a grocery store
- the playground
- the backyard
- your bedroom
- an amusement park
- a sporting event
- the beach
- the mall
- the kitchen
- an art class
- a museum
- a restaurant
- in a car
- on a bus
- a family reunion
- a farm
- your best friend's home

8. Point out the suitcases and ask if students have seen a television show *(Deal or No Deal)* that has a similar array of briefcases, or other game shows where prizes are hidden behind a door. Explain that these cases contain the names of valuable vacation trips or places to visit. Students are to imagine traveling to each place and to think of a way they might use the new vocabulary word in that setting.

9. Select a student to come up, open the suitcase of his choice, and read aloud the trip location named inside.

10. Direct students to work in pairs. Explain that each pair is to develop a sentence that would be an appropriate use of the new word in the chosen location. Examples from a social studies unit might include:

    Allegiance, in the grocery store: "My allegiance is to Cocoa Puffer cereal."

    Regulate, on the playground: "Sara and I had to regulate the softball game before it got out of hand."

    Nation, in the kitchen: "We have foods from many nations in our cupboards."

11. Change what is written on the insides of the suitcases from time to time to infuse some unpredictability.

Additional Ideas

* Label the Idea Suitcases with the names of various occupations. Students can generate ideas for how someone with that job might use the vocabulary word in his line of work.

* Write the names of cartoon characters and superheroes on the insides of the cases. Ask students to consider how these individuals might use the word.

* Use Idea Suitcases to support the math curriculum, too. Place a gold star in one of the cases. Have students figure out the odds of choosing the suitcase with the star. Each time a suitcase is opened, students can calculate the odds of finding the star with the next selection.

Reflections

How did the students respond? What evidence do you have that the strategy was successful? Are there adaptations to the strategy that you might try in the future? Other thoughts?

_____

_____

_____

_____

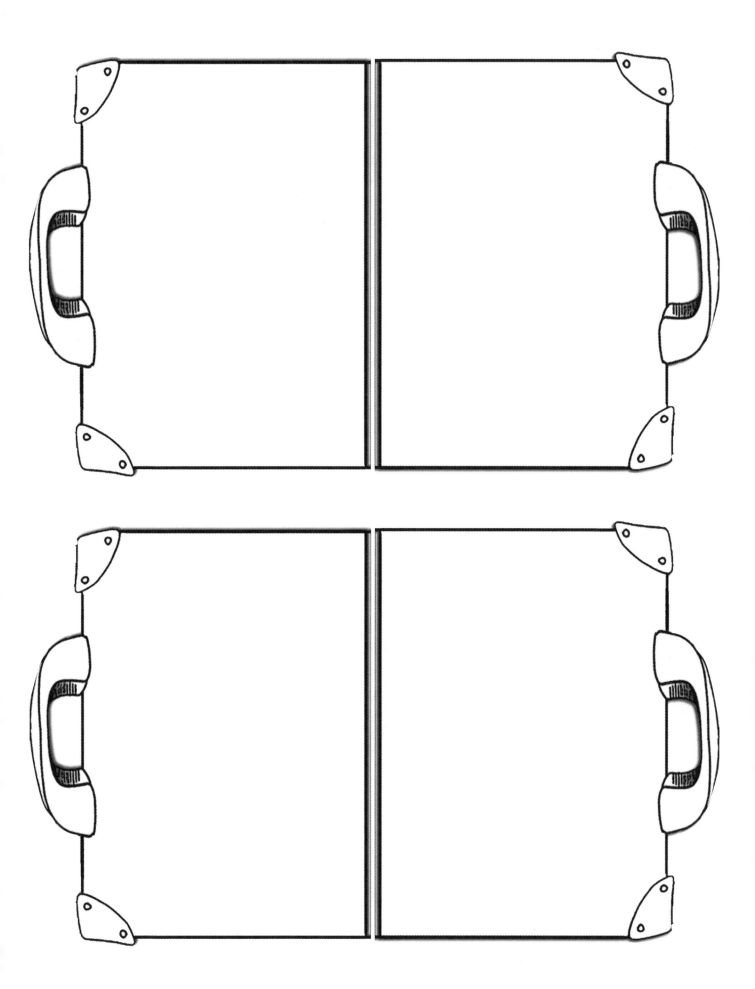

BEST PRACTICE

Determining Importance

It's a warm summer day, and most of the windows in the house are open. Before leaving for your dinner out, you check the sky for clouds. You look westward to where the storms usually arrive on the horizon. All is clear and the sky is calm. You decide that, although thunderstorms are common at this time of year, it is safe to leave the windows open for a few hours while you are gone. You have just used several cognitive processes to determine your course of action.

Activating prior knowledge is a cognitive process used so frequently in our day-to-day lives that it becomes an unconscious process. We use it to make sense of new information, to determine critical or important things to focus our attention on, to make predictions about the future, and to plan our actions. Our attempts at predicting, or saying what is going to happen in the future, are typically most accurate when they have a basis in knowledge or past experience.

The process of generating predictions or hypotheses helps students become aware of their own knowledge base and determine the value of various pieces of knowledge in a given situation (Cooper and Levine, 2008). It has also been shown to have a significant impact on student achievement. Hypothesizing is considered a high-yield activity during and after a learning experience because it engages students in analyzing, applying, and reassessing their knowledge (Marzano, 2003).

Reflective Questions

- Identify a prediction you made today. What factors went into your making that prediction?
- What factors do students most likely use when making their own predictions?
- Predictions are common in reading and science labs. What other activities during the week lend themselves to encouraging students to make predictions?

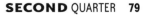

Idea for Daily Practice

Forever Fortune Cookies

Fortune cookies are considered an entertaining way to end a meal, by combining something sweet with a forecast of what the future has to bring. Most students are familiar with the heightened anticipation associated with cracking open the cookie, pulling out the miniature piece of paper, and reading the fortune. The same anticipation is present in classrooms when you use Forever Fortune Cookies. These reusable, easy-to-make containers can hold predictions or hypotheses and will definitely hold students' attention!

Materials

6 sheets of tan craft foam

Glue gun

Slips of 1 x 4-inch paper

How To

1. Cut 4-inch-diameter circles out of the craft foam.

2. Fold a circle in half and place a dab of hot glue inside each end of the fold line. Press until dry. (In the illustration, "x" marks the spot.)

3. Bend the semicircle along the fold so that it forms an arch, with the two ends of the fold coming together in the middle. Apply a dab of hot glue and press until dry. You have completed your first fortune cookie.

4. Repeat until you have one cookie for each student.

5. In class, generate a brief discussion about fortune cookies by asking students if they have ever eaten fortune cookies. Talk about the types of fortunes they might have found inside. Weave the words *prediction* and *hypothesis* into your discussion, helping students to clarify the differences between them.

6. Discuss and record the factors that lead to a good prediction or hypothesis. These might include the words *if* and *then*. Older students might generate words such as *related to, testable,* or *independent and dependent variables.*

7. Provide each student with a Forever Fortune Cookie and a slip of paper. Introduce the lesson and ask each student to write a prediction on his paper. For example, when starting a new novel, show the students the cover, review the title, do a picture walk, and then ask the students to predict what the story will be about. In a science unit, provide a basic overview of the experiment and ask students to develop a hypothesis.

8. Once the predictions have been completed, have students slip them into the Forever Fortune Cookies.

9. When cookies are complete have students work in pairs. Direct partners to swap cookies and read each other's predictions, discussing the differences and explaining their rationale. Then proceed with the lesson to see who had accurate predictions.

Additional Ideas

◈ Because Forever Fortune Cookies are made of foam, they can be used over and over again. Have students use the cookies when they predict how they will perform on a spelling test or when they estimate how many jelly beans are in a jar. Or pull out the cookies again when students guess who will win the World Series, based on sports statistics.

◈ Use cookies made of different colors of foam to represent different areas of the curriculum.

Reflections

How did the students respond? What evidence do you have that the strategy was successful? Are there adaptations to the strategy that you might try in the future? Other thoughts?

BEST PRACTICE

Strengthening Memory

The school day is filled to overflowing with teacher-led instruction, cooperative learning, activities, practice, assessment, and so much more. It often feels like there is not enough time for everything! Yet as full as the school day is, some students still need more time to learn the basic concepts. Keeping students after school is not always a viable solution, so how can we increase student learning without adding minutes to the day?

In studying memory, researchers have identified two different ways of learning simple facts—one is *implicit* learning and the other is *explicit* learning. Implicit learning occurs when a person is exposed to new material indirectly, and the information is later moved into long-term memory as it's related to other knowledge. Explicit learning occurs through directed attention to specific material; it's a more conscious process.

Brain imaging studies have shown that during learning, blood flow in specific areas of the brain increases less if implicit learning precedes explicit learning. Researchers suggest two potential conclusions from this data. The first is that if implicit learning occurs before explicit learning, the memory trace is activated with greater efficiency, requiring less blood flow. The second theory is that it takes less attention and effort to recall and respond to information that we have previously encountered than it does to react to material that is brand new to us (Posner and Rothbart, 2007). Both of these theories offer clues that we can use to strengthen student memory and boost learning.

Researchers at McMaster University in Hamilton, Ontario, have been studying the effects on children of implicit exposure to music. Their findings suggest that children who grow up listening to music in the home develop a brain response similar to that of a child two years older who has not had that advantage (Society for Neuroscience, 2003).

Similarly, background listening is a key component of the Suzuki approach to music instruction. Teachers have found that students who listen to their musical pieces while doing other things learn to play those pieces more quickly and more accurately.

The educational implication is that you may be able to make learning more time efficient if you can provide your students with implicit exposure to new material prior to giving direct instruction. The challenge is to find additional instructional moments in an already-full day.

Reflective Questions

- What skills have you learned by first having implicit exposure to new material?
- What percentage of student learning time is spent on implicit exposure versus explicit learning?

• When are there moments throughout the school week when you might be able to build in some implicit exposure to concepts without taking away from all the necessary things already scheduled?

_____

_____

_____

_____

_____

Idea for Daily Practice

Spelling CD

> "Listening to the spelling words helped me learn my words faster."
>
> —AJ T.

Correct spelling involves many skills—including sound-symbol connections, phonemic manipulation, word segmenting, memorization, and the ability to recognize patterns. Effective literacy and word study programs incorporate all of these skills into their weekly lessons. You can increase your effectiveness as a teacher by giving your students implicit exposure to weekly spelling words through an auditory CD recording.

Materials

List of spelling words

1 blank CD and a CD player or computer with audio recording capabilities

How To

1. Select the spelling words, or word study list, for the coming week.

2. Record the words on an audio CD, or record them directly onto a computer with recording capabilities. In either case, state each word and then spell it three times in succession. Choose a pace appropriate for your students' ability level; lists of 10 words usually take between two and three minutes.

3. Consider your daily schedule. Think of a time when the Spelling CD could be playing in the background as students are doing something else. Suitable times might be as students are arriving in class and putting away their materials, as they are writing in their planners, as they are lining up for lunch, or as they pack up to go home. (Remember that the recording probably will be only two to three minutes long.)

4. Explain to students that they will be hearing their new spelling words in the background as they are completing other tasks. Clarify that they do not need to change their behaviors in any way during this time. However, if they want to lip-synch with the recording, they can do so!

5. Starting a day or two prior to giving out the spelling lists, play the Spelling CD once each day. Do the same thing again on the days when students are studying that particular list of words.

Additional Ideas

☀ Seek out a high school student in need of community service hours and ask her to record the CDs for you. Or approach the National Honor Society and ask that group to take on this project for your entire school.

☀ Consider other information that might lend itself to a recording playing in the background. Math facts, vocabulary and definitions, and the periodic table of elements are examples of content that require rote memorization that can be supported through auditory recordings.

☀ Collaborate with the technology specialist in your school to develop a spelling video to place on the school Web site. Each week a different group of students can be chosen to design a creative way to present the spelling words. Ask a parent volunteer to videotape the students and upload the video to the Web site. Remind students to click in from home to watch their peers and prime themselves to study the new words (or other new content).

Reflections

How did the students respond? What evidence do you have that the strategy was successful? Are there adaptations to the strategy that you might try in the future? Other thoughts?

BEST PRACTICE

Summarizing

"The search for meaning is innate." These powerful words by Caine and Caine summarize what much of the research and our own personal learning experience tells us—that humans are wired to try to make sense of things in their lives. The search for meaning often involves culling essential elements from a new experience and finding connections with something familiar. When this process involves "thoughts, emotions, senses, and the entire body, it goes beyond the physiology of the brain alone and becomes felt sense (Caine, R. and G.; McClintic; and Klimek; 2009)."

The ability to cull the main ideas of a new passage or lecture and weave them into a summary statement is an outward demonstration of comprehension. Research shows that teachers can boost comprehension by using stimulating tasks to arouse attention (Guthrie, Wigfield, and Humenick; 2006). Situations that focus attention by eliciting mild to moderate emotion are powerful stimuli for learning. In those instances, the brain releases neurotransmitters such as dopamine and acetylcholine in just the right amounts to activate the critical learning centers in the brain (Caine, R. and G.; McClintic; and Klimek; 2008). When students' emotions are involved in the learning process, their comprehension improves; they become more capable of generating effective summaries and retaining key information.

Reflective Questions

- What moods or emotions do you notice in yourself during a peak learning experience?
- What connections do you see between your students' emotions and their ability to comprehend or summarize?
- How can you weave positive emotions into summarizing activities so that your students improve their summarization skills and retain their new learning better?

Idea for Daily Practice

Human Machines

When students deeply comprehend material, they can summarize their learning in a variety of ways. The Human Machines strategy is an enactment opportunity that uses cognition, emotion, and movement to capture the main idea of the learning and burn it into memory (Wilhelm, 2002). As the learning becomes visible through the use of motion and emotion, both the performers and the observers are viscerally affected, gaining a "felt sense" of their new knowledge.

Materials

None!

How To

1. Ask students to share aloud examples of machines. Lead students in identifying common characteristics of machines. Be sure that "noise" and "moving parts" are listed as two main characteristics.

2. Explain to students that they will have the opportunity to enact emotions and themes, concepts that are usually abstract, by building a concrete Human Machine. Identify two or three main characteristics of machines—such as noise and motion—that must be present in the enactment.

3. Choose an emotion or theme that is an important main idea of the material being studied. For example, if the class is reading the classic novel *Fahrenheit 451,* by Ray Bradbury (1953), it would be appropriate to emphasize paranoia or censorship. Or, in the well-loved children's book *The Keeping Quilt,* by Patricia Polacco (1988), you could stress the passing down of traditions.

4. Pick three volunteers to build a machine. The first student will stand in front of the class and begin making a motion and a noise of some kind to represent the theme (for example, paranoia). After three to five seconds, direct the second student to link onto the first student (the machine) and add her own motion and sound. After another three to five seconds, ask the third student to join in, physically linking himself to the machine and adding his motion and sound. After a few more seconds have passed, pause the machine.

5. Ask students to react to what they observed in the human machine. Students might start by talking to partners, then offer comments to the whole group. Reflective questions might include, "How did the level of intensity match your sense of the novel?" and "What other motions or noises might depict this concept?"

Additional Ideas

☼ Group students into trios and assign each trio a concept or emotion to depict to the class through the Human Machines strategy.

☼ Secretly inform the Human Machine volunteers of the concept they are to depict. Ask the rest of the class to guess the concept after observing the enactment.

☼ Use the Human Machines strategy before reading to encourage students to be on the lookout for specific emotions or abstract ideas.

☼ Ask all students to close their eyes and visualize a machine representing an abstract idea that is part of the lesson. For example, students might imagine what a democracy machine would look and sound like. Then have students share their ideas.

Reflections

How did the students respond? What evidence do you have that the strategy was successful? Are there adaptations to the strategy that you might try in the future? Other thoughts?

BEST PRACTICE

Challenging Thinking

Successful students have effective cognitive structures through which they process the information they receive in school each day. Cognitive structures include a variety of mental processes, such as making connections, identifying patterns and relationships, and abstract thinking. Struggling students often have underdeveloped cognitive structures (Garner, 2007). Unfortunately, you can't teach these structures directly—instead, you must act as a facilitator for the student as he develops them on his own. Many a frustrated parent or teacher has exclaimed, "I taught it. I just don't know why he didn't get it!"

Connections and relationships allow individual students to integrate new information into their own existing schema. Connections that work for a teacher or other adult may not have personal meaning for a student who has had different experiences. Relationships or patterns between things that you point out might result in imitation by a student, but may not lead to true understanding and transfer of learning. Students need to construct meaning for themselves (Brooks, J. and M.; 1993). It usually feels as if you are conveying information more quickly when you provide direct instruction to students—"telling"—but this may not be as effective as allowing students to take a bit more time and find out for themselves. When you facilitate opportunities for students to explore and create connections on their own, you facilitate higher levels of thinking.

Reflective Questions

- What strategies do you use to integrate new information with your existing knowledge and experience?
- Do you sometimes rush students or cut short the time they need to process information because of feeling pressured to get through your curriculum agenda?
- Is there one time during the day when you could extend the time students have to make meaning for themselves?

Idea for Daily Practice

Mystery Box

> "The Mystery Box was like a close baseball game, and you're waiting for what's going to happen next."
> —Noah T.

Mysteries quickly engage our curiosity and activate higher-level thinking skills. Many mysteries—novels, science experiments, television crime shows—are complicated and involve lots of factors. But busy teachers need simple ideas for the classroom. Mystery Boxes are simple! These boxes provide students with an unknown object and a challenge to create a connection to the lesson. Easily applied to any lesson content, Mystery Boxes result in creative, advanced applications from students who are ready for a challenge.

Materials

1 box with lid

A variety of small, everyday items

Reproducible #13

A journal or notebook

How To

1. Make one copy of the reproducible.

2. Cut a hole in the top of the box lid. Make it large enough for a student's hand to fit through, but not so large that it is easy to see inside. If desired, partially cover the hole with jagged paper, as in the illustration, to make it more difficult for students to see inside.

3. Place a variety of small, everyday items inside the box. The greater the variety and randomness, the better!

4. Paste the Mystery Box directions to the front of the box.

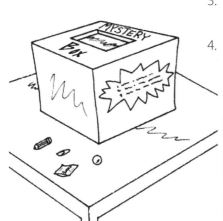

Possible Items for the Mystery Box

- pencil stub
- paperclip
- pad of sticky notes
- small rubber ball
- miniature toys
- sugar packet
- piece of yarn
- plastic toothpaste lid
- rubber band

5. Explain to students that throughout the week, they will have a chance to use the Mystery Box. Review the directions with the students and model the expected behavior. Reach into the box and pull something out. Relate it to a lesson concept of the day or week. For example, if the class has been studying metric conversion and you pull out a pencil stub, think aloud as you create a way to relate the pencil stub to metrics ("I could use it for a measuring stick and mark metric on one side and standard on the other" or "A pencil stub compared to a full-size pencil is like a centimeter compared to a decimeter.") Ask the students for additional ideas. If students are studying the creation of the American political system and the item pulled from the box is a rubber band, the connection might be: "The founding fathers wanted a political system with a little bit of give or stretch so that as times changed, the system could be responsive."

6. Tell students that you will leave a notebook with the Mystery Box so that they can write down in the notebook the connections they create.

7. Place the box and notebook in an accessible place. Throughout the week direct one or two students at a time to work with the Mystery Box to make connections or create relationships.

Additional Ideas

☼ Save a few minutes at the end of a lesson to use the Mystery Box with the whole class. Ask for a student volunteer to pull something out of the box. Direct each student to turn to a nearby peer and create a connection together. Encourage students to share their ideas with the whole class.

☼ Ask students to bring you small items from home that they feel would be right for the Mystery Box.

Reflections

How did the students respond? What evidence do you have that the strategy was successful? Are there adaptations to the strategy that you might try in the future? Other thoughts?

_____

_____

_____

_____

1. **Pull something out of the box (without looking!)**

2. **Think of a way that you could do something with the item that would involve the concept you are learning about.**

3. **Put the item back in the box.**

Third Quarter

BEST PRACTICE

Increasing Participation

"Students who watch interesting and engaging activities that others do, but are not actively participating, are not likely to show an enrichment response. Students must actually do it (2006)!" These words, from researcher and educator Eric Jensen, serve as a challenge to teachers everywhere to evaluate the level of active engagement in their classrooms. Jensen's review of the brain research led him to conclude that "brain enrichment," or brain growth, is a result of a variety of factors that include physical activity, meaningful learning opportunities, and social support. The old model of "sit and listen" to the teacher lecture is not supported by the rapidly growing number of studies on effective learning.

In today's classrooms, student voices are beginning to be heard. While some teachers continue to dominate the talk in a class, most recognize the value of engaging learners in active discussion of the content. "Allowing students to voice an opinion or insight, or make personal connections to the content, makes them part of a group that helps to define knowledge (Allen, 2008)." And in addition to engaging learners more fully, student-centered discussion provides an opportunity for you to assess levels of understanding and provide targeted prompts.

However, because discussions rely heavily on the auditory modality, you might need to take additional steps to engage all students. Students who are in the early levels of learning English as a second language need tactile and kinesthetic supports (Haynes, 2007). Piggybacking is an especially effective way to add on to conversational threads and extend understanding for students whose language skills are still developing. Strategic tools can provide a safe path by which struggling students can enter discussions and participate more with the necessary supports (Paxton-Buursma and Walker, 2008).

Reflective Questions

- What do you do to stay engaged when you find yourself expected to listen for a lengthy period? To participate in a lengthy discussion?
- How much of the school day is teacher led vs. student led?
- What opportunities exist during the week to increase student discussion?

Idea for Daily Practice

I'm In!

Book discussion groups, or literacy circles, are a popular approach to engaging students in active discussions about books they are reading. You may already use a variety of tools to structure these discussions while still striving for authentic discourse; here is another one you may want to add to your repertoire. The I'm In! strategy is a simple yet effective tool for increasing students' motivation to participate and simultaneously providing discussion prompts that make it easier for them to participate. You provide students with I'm In! poker chips that have graphic cues related to a variety of reading strategies they have been taught. You then encourage them to toss a poker chip into a container when they have something to say. The similarity to playing poker adds a game-like quality that enhances student participation.

Materials

Reproducible #14

Plastic poker chips (optional)

1 paper plate or container per group

How To

1. Make one copy of the reproducible for each student. Laminate the pieces and cut them apart.

2. if desired, adhere each laminated piece to the top of a poker chip.

3. Ask students if they have ever played poker. Describe how poker players must choose to participate by calling "I'm in" and tossing poker chips into the middle of the table. Share phrases such as "get your head in the game" or "I'm really into skateboarding."

4. Distribute a set of chips to each student.

5. Discuss the reading strategy represented by each I'm In! poker chip. Remind students of how effective readers use these strategies to increase their comprehension and enjoyment of a book.

6. Explain to students that when one of them is ready to participate in the book discussion, he is to call "I'm in" and toss onto the plate a poker chip that represents the comment or question he would like to make. For example, if a student wants to piggyback on another student's insight, he should toss in the "pig" poker chip.

7. Arrange students into book discussion groups. If all students are reading the same material, then mixed-ability groups will work best. If students are reading different-leveled novels then you may want to create more homogenous groups. Direct each group of students to sit in a circle and place the container in the center of the circle.

8. Monitor students as they engage in discussion. If you notice a student has not put in a poker chip, ask her to look at the pictures on the chips to help her think of something to add.

9. If desired, have students pause halfway through the discussion period and reflect on how "in the game" they are.

10. With a few minutes remaining in the lesson period, ask students to reflect on which chips were used and which were not. (Not every reading selection lends itself to all of the reading strategies on the chips.) Guide discussion about ways to "stay in the game."

Additional Ideas

❀ For other lessons that lend themselves to student discussion, design symbols that represent the types of contributions you would like students to make. For example, during a science lesson, you might have symbols that represent hypothesis, procedure, observation, results, and conclusion.

❀ Students can use plain poker chips to participate in discussions that do not lend themselves to a predetermined set of contributions.

❀ If students have not yet been exposed to all of the I'm In! reading strategies, provide them with just a few of the most familiar chips.

Reflections

How did the students respond? What evidence do you have that the strategy was successful? Are there adaptations to the strategy that you might try in the future? Other thoughts?

_____

_____

_____

_____

_____

Predicting

Clarifying

Piggybacking

Summarizing

Feeling

Visualizing

Connecting

Questioning

Vocabulary

Focusing Attention

Effective readers frequently read a section of text several times, with different purposes each time. Perkins-Gough, a well-known literacy expert, explains, "Rereading with a purpose is perhaps the most vital strategy for promoting both fluency and deep understanding of texts in every discipline (2002)." Many students need explicit instruction on how to read, or reread, with a specific purpose in mind. When you can pair this instruction with a tool that makes reading a tactile endeavor, students who learn best through tactile or kinesthetic means will be more engaged in what is traditionally a visual and auditory activity.

Reflective Questions

- When you are rereading for a specific purpose, how do you keep yourself focused on that purpose?
- When you ask your students to reread a text, what are some of the purposes you suggest to them?
- How can you encourage students to reread even when they are not required by you to do so at that moment?

Idea for Daily Practice

Purposeful Reading Tool

Color is commonly used to focus our attention—think of yellow hazard lights, bright advertisements, neon "sale" stickers. Color can be an effective means for focusing student attention in the classroom, too. The Purposeful Reading Tool (similar to the Writer's Revision Tool) is a color-coded, hands-on tool that assists students in becoming more focused or purposeful in their reading. Flexible enough to be adapted for different curricula and different grade levels, the Purposeful Reading Tool provides color-coded reminders of four key text elements chosen by the teacher. Color, combined with tactile input, is a sure-fire way to boost your students' attention.

Materials

Reproducible #15

Cardstock

2 sheets of acetate in each of four colors (red, blue, green, and yellow)

Tape

How To

1. Choose four purposes of rereading that are appropriate for the level of your students. Write each purpose along one edge of the tool, on the blank line provided. These characteristics might include things such as new vocabulary, key events, important details, names, dates, or main ideas.

2. Make one copy of the reproducible, on cardstock, for every two students.

3. If desired, laminate the rectangles for greater durability.

4. Cut the acetate into 1-inch strips.

5. Working with one tool at a time, tape one strip of colored acetate to the back of each edge, allowing approximately two-thirds of the strip to clear the edge. Use each of the four colors on each tool, being careful to see that the colors and corresponding purpose are the same on all the tools you make.

6. When students will be reading a common text, distribute the tools. Explain to students that sometimes it is important to reread a text with a specific purpose in mind.

7. Model for students how to slide the Purposeful Reading Tool down a page, one sentence at a time, looking through the acetate for a specific type of information. For example, if red corresponds to new vocabulary, have students look at each line through the red acetate, searching for unknown words. If they find one, they should stop and mark the word with a sticky note or write it down on scrap paper so that they remember to look up its meaning.

8. After they scan the text for one purpose, show the students how to turn the tool so that another color and purpose are at the top, and have them repeat Step #7.

Additional Idea

✹ Use the blank side of the tool to customize the purposes of reading based on your current lesson. For example, if you are teaching students about parts of speech, the tool might be labeled for nouns, verbs, adjectives, and adverbs. Write the labels on the board with different colored markers to correspond with the colored acetate strips. Then have students transfer the labels to their tools using wet- or dry-erase markers.

Reflections

How did the students respond? What evidence do you have that the strategy was successful? Are there adaptations to the strategy that you might try in the future? Other thoughts?

_____

_____

_____

_____

_____

Purposeful Reading Tool

Purposeful Reading Tool

Identifying Similarities & Differences

The Venn diagram was introduced by John Venn in 1880 as a way to visually represent the logical relationships between sets. Widely used in schools today, it is employed to help students look at similarities and differences between two events, concepts, stories, or items. Venn diagrams have also been shown to improve students' literal and relational comprehension (DiCecco and Gleason, 2002).

While Venn diagrams work well at sorting most things, they do have their limitations. They are not the best tools, for example, for dealing with outliers. In mathematics, an *outlier* is defined as an observation that is numerically distant from the rest of the data. Outliers exist in other curricular areas as well; they may be referred to as anomalies, irregularities, or hiccups. Outliers can generate meaty conversation as students analyze, compare, and decide what fits in a group and what does not. But Venn diagrams tend to focus on sets with multiple items, so they are not sensitive tools for dealing with outliers.

Venn diagrams and similar sorting devices are also limited by the fact that they *only* emphasize the representation of relationships visually. Visual cues are extremely effective for some students, but when you involve multiple modalities in a lesson, you are likely to enhance learning significantly. "The most effective instructional techniques unite the mind and the body (Tate, 2006)." With this in mind, effective teachers look for ways to link verbal, visual, and tactile cues together for a potent learning experience.

Reflective Questions

- What non-work related experiences do you encounter that require you to discern similarities and differences between two or more things?
- Which of your students seem to struggle with sorting things into categories? What might be the root cause of their struggle?
- What opportunities exist throughout the school day for students to identify similarities and differences of two or more things?

Idea for Daily Practice

Bottle-Cap Sort

With tight classroom budgets, ideas that don't cost anything are very attractive to teachers. Fortunately, Bottle-Cap Sort is also a strategy that is attractive to students! This instructional strategy uses the plastic caps from water bottles to practice skills used in identifying similarities and differences. You can use wet-erase markers to mark the caps with words, numbers, letters, or colors and then give them to students to sort. Students can move the caps around on a table or desk top, or sort them using a Styrofoam sorting board for even greater tactile input. So ask your students to help you collect these bottle caps, and before you know it you'll have more than you need! (A quick tip: Organized events like fun runs, fairs, or soccer games are great places to collect bottle caps!)

Materials

At least 130 clear plastic bottle caps from recyclable water bottles

1 square of 1/2-inch-thick Styrofoam, approximately 12 x 12 inches, for every four students (optional)

Wet-erase markers

How To

1. If using the Styrofoam, score 64 circles into one of the squares by gently pushing the caps into place in an 8 x 8 pattern. (If you prefer, you can skip this step and have students sort the caps without using a board.)

2. Generate a demonstration set of bottle caps by writing a word on each cap with a wet-erase marker. For instance, the words might represent nouns, verbs, and adjectives. (In a science class, the caps might have relevant abbreviations for the Periodic Table of Elements.)

3. Using your demonstration set of bottle tops, show students how the caps can be sorted into sets based on their parts of speech. Twist the caps into different sections of the board to show the three sets.

4. Provide each student with one blank bottle cap and a marker. Direct him to write a short word that is a noun, verb, or adjective on the top of his cap. When ready, have students add these caps to the sorting board, talking about their decisions as they place the caps in sets.

5. Divide students into groups of four. Provide each group with approximately 20 blank bottle caps and a sorting board.

6. Give students directions about what to write on their bottle tops, depending on your instructional objective. For example:

   - Nonsense words for a lesson on vowel patterns
   - Nouns (or verbs, adjectives, etc.) for a lesson on parts of speech
   - Numerals for a lesson on multiples
   - Numbers for complex pattern puzzles (e.g., *2, 7, 57, 3250, ???*)

7. Encourage students to work collaboratively to sort the bottle caps into sets that have similar characteristics. Suggest that they may find an outlier that will take a space by itself. Wander around the classroom and provide guidance as necessary.

8. Pull the class back together. Ask students to hold up their sorting boards and explain the reasoning behind their decisions.

Additional Ideas

☼ Create temporary Venn diagram circles on your sorting board or work surface with Wikki Stix or yarn.

☼ Use sorting boards to sequence letters into alphabetical order, numbers into numerical order, or days of the week into calendar order.

☼ Write letters on bottle caps and have students use them to practice spelling words.

☼ Write students' initials on bottle tops. Have students talk about the ways in which classmates are similar and different (height, hair color, gender, age, number of siblings, and so on).

☼ When a student makes a connection or participates in a desired way, ask her to place a cap on the board. Encourage students to make patterns or shapes as they add more caps to the board.

Reflections

How did the students respond? What evidence do you have that the strategy was successful? Are there adaptations to the strategy that you might try in the future? Other thoughts?

_____

_____

_____

_____

_____

BEST PRACTICE

Using Non-Linguistic Representations

Visualization, the process of creating vivid mental images of something, has been used in many fields to improve performance and productivity. Neurologists tell us that the act of visualizing helps us to form new patterns and connections in multiple regions of the brain. This can result in an increased release of dopamine and serotonin (neurotransmitters) that reinforces synaptic connections (Willis, 2007). In other words, visualization leads to stronger learning connections for students!

Reflective Questions

- What have been your personal experiences with visualization?
- How do you currently use visualization in your teaching? How effective has it been?
- Throughout the week, what teaching and learning opportunities exist in which students would benefit from visualization?

Idea for Daily Practice

Director's Clapboard

"'Lights, camera, action' helped me with putting detail in my writing. Now I'm one of the strongest writers in the class!"
–Makenzie L.

Visualizing is a skill for which many students need direct instruction. The Director's Clapboard strategy, which asks students to direct their own movie, gives you a way to provide that instruction while tapping into the enthusiasm most students demonstrate for movies. The strategy provides students with directed practice in effectively visualizing a scene. It can be used in conjunction with a writing task, as in the following example, but it is also helpful for visualizing a word problem in math, a time period in history, or the use of a conflict-resolution strategy. Simple director's clapboards are available from several web-based party supply stores.

Materials

Director's clapboard

Reproducible #16

Black construction paper

Glue sticks

How To

1. Make one copy of the reproducible for each student.

2. Grab the students' attention by telling them that they will be making movies today.

3. Reveal the Director's Clapboard strategy, explaining that movie directors use a clapboard to indicate the starting point of a new scene. When the clap is heard on a movie set, action begins.

4. Explain to the students that the movies they make will be in their heads. You will lead them to picture, or visualize, what a scene looks like in great detail.

5. Direct the students to close their eyes when they hear the clap of the clapboard.

6. Begin by announcing "Lights, camera, action," and then clapping the board. If necessary, remind students to close their eyes and keep them closed.

7. Read a simple statement to the class. For example, you might read, "The woman was in the kitchen cooking." Follow the statement with questions designed to help the students visualize the scene. Questions might include:

- What does the woman look like? How old is she? What is the color of her skin? Her hair? Is she tall? Skinny?
- Where is the woman standing in the kitchen? Is she by the sink? The stove? The counter?
- What is the woman doing? Is she chopping? Stirring? Pouring?
- Is there anyone else in the kitchen with her?
- What is she cooking?
- What do you smell? What sounds do you hear?

8. When you have allowed sufficient time for processing, call out "Cut!" and ask the students to open their eyes. Call on students to share what they pictured in their scenes.

9. Repeat the process for additional practice, using simple statements that represent situations familiar to students. Avoid including a lot of detail in the practice sentence.

10. Give each student a copy of the reproducible and a sheet of black construction paper. Have students cut and paste the reproducible—including all the lines for responses—onto the construction paper so that each student has her own clapboard.

11. Instruct each student to write his name on the "Director" line of his reproducible, since he will be directing his own movie. On the "Production" line, have each student write a sentence from a sample of his own writing that he believes could be more descriptive. Depending on the students' ages, this might be a sentence with a dead or passive verb, one without any adjectives, or one with words that are overused in student writing (such as *said, good, fun, nice, went*). If necessary, help individual students find appropriate sentences.

12. Use the Director's Clapboard to initiate the visualization process, as in Step #6. After students have closed their eyes, prompt them to picture in their minds what the scene looks like in detail. Suggest they think of sounds, smells, actions, colors, sizes, and so on. After sufficient time has passed, direct students to open their eyes; explain that each student should write her "scene," an improved sentence, on the reproducible. For example, an original sentence might have been, "My family went on a vacation." The improved sentence, after visualizing, might say, "As the Turner family pulled up to the sandy beach, the four excited children rushed to be the first out of the steamy station wagon."

Additional Ideas

- Once students have practiced the Director's Clapboard strategy, you can recall it quickly by prompting the students with the phrase "Lights, camera, action" and clapping your hands. This simple approach is helpful for on-the-spot use such as during read-alouds, when solving word problems, and in discussions that encourage predictions.

- After practicing as a whole group, you may want students to practice in small groups before moving to independent work.

- Store the clapboard in a spot where it can be seen easily. As students engage in individual writing assignments, remind them to scan the room for resources and helpful reminders. Reinforce the idea that the clapboard is their reminder to visualize before they write.

- Provide each group with a clapboard and a piece of chalk. Allow students to write their scene descriptions directly onto the clapboard.

Reflections

How did the students respond? What evidence do you have that the strategy was successful? Are there adaptations to the strategy that you might try in the future? Other thoughts?

HOllYWOOD
PRODUCTION_____

DIRECTOR_____

_____

_____

_____

_____

_____

_____

DATE	SCENE	TAKE

BEST PRACTICE

Making Connections

Picture a large city during rush hour. You are trying to get across town, but there is a three-car crash blocking your normal route. You quickly transition into the turn lane and thank your lucky stars that you know an alternate route, smiling as you view the traffic jam in your rearview mirror.

Competent adults utilize connections in every walk of life. (Even the fact that you can relate this driving metaphor to teaching shows your skill at making a successful connection!) Very successful adults, the "gifted," have developed these skills to an even higher level and can more quickly process the connections they make. By tapping into our existing knowledge and applying what we already know to new concepts and ideas, we become "neurally efficient" and can acquire new, complex information more quickly (Jensen, 2006).

K-W-L charts, originally designed by Donna Ogle (1986), are a powerful tool for encouraging students to identify what they already know about a topic; activating prior knowledge helps learners to absorb new content in a more meaningful way. While most often used as a literacy strategy, activating prior knowledge is also "at the heart of doing mathematics (Hyde, 2007)." In fact, activating prior knowledge makes good sense in all curriculum areas!

Reflective Questions

- During the past week, were there any moments when you consciously activated your prior knowledge about something?
- What methods do you currently use to have students activate their prior knowledge about a new topic?
- Do your current strategies appear to work for all your students?

_____

_____

_____

_____

_____

Idea for Daily Practice

Lighting Up the Brain

"I never knew I had electricity in my brain. Now I try harder than ever to have more and more sparks and zaps."

—Mark K.

Typically, K-W-L charts and other strategies for activating knowledge use an auditory or visual modality. But culturally responsive, inclusive classrooms need to incorporate movement as well in order to create effective learning environments for all students (Boykin, Tyler, Watkins-Lewis, and Kizzie; 2006) (Payne, 2008). Lighting Up the Brain is a strategy that actively engages students in sharing their subject knowledge and also teaches students that their brain activity increases when they make personal connections. As a result, all students are highly motivated to participate because they want to see the luminous final outcome.

Materials

1 six-foot piece of brown butcher paper

1 marker for each student

1 bottle of glow-in-the-dark paint

1 paintbrush

Reproducible #17

How To

1. Draw an outline of a brain on the butcher paper. Label the paper, "Our Class's Brain." Set it aside.

2. Make a copy of the reproducible.

3. Show students your copy of the reproducible. Explain that brain researchers have determined that areas of the brain in which we process many things we think about can't yet be pinpointed. Point out various labels on the brain map. Explain to students that you will be asking them to make connections between their prior knowledge and the new topic. If they want to, they can look at the labels on the brain map to help them generate ideas. Extend the discussion to include the fact that the brain is constantly generating electrical impulses, and that those impulses increase as thinking increases.

4. Place the butcher-paper brain on the floor and have students sit around the edges of the paper. Provide each student with a marker.

5. Announce the new topic that the class is about to study. For example, "Today we are going to begin a unit on the solar system. Start thinking about what you already know about the solar system—anything at all! If you get stuck trying to think of something, look at the brain map to help you out." Allow some quiet think time.

6. Choose a student to share something he knows about the topic. After he shares with the group, direct him to write his idea onto the "class brain." When he is finished, ask him to dab a large dot of glow-in-the-dark paint next to his statement.

7. Continue choosing students to participate at a rate that sustains attention and high engagement. You may want to have one student sharing verbally while another is still writing or painting.

8. When students have finished sharing, close any blinds and turn off the lights. Watch the excitement as the class "brain" lights up with dozens of glowing dots!

Additional Ideas

❋ If floor space is limited, students can work on chart paper on the wall. This also works well for older students if they are less comfortable sitting on the floor.

❋ Students can make individual "brains" by writing a variety of connections on plain paper or on crinkled, brown-paper lunch bags and painting glow-in-the-dark dots on the surface. If paint is not available, each student can place a flashlight inside her bag and turn it on to illuminate spots on the surface.

❋ When drawing the large "brain" onto butcher paper, section off portions and label them to indicate different concepts. For example, sections might be labeled "What We Know," "What We Want to Know," and "What We Learned."

❋ Provide each student with a copy of the reproducible and have her write connections directly on the brain map. She can then store her map in a notebook and update it at the end of the unit.

Reflections

How did the students respond? What evidence do you have that the strategy was successful? Are there adaptations to the strategy that you might try in the future? Other thoughts?

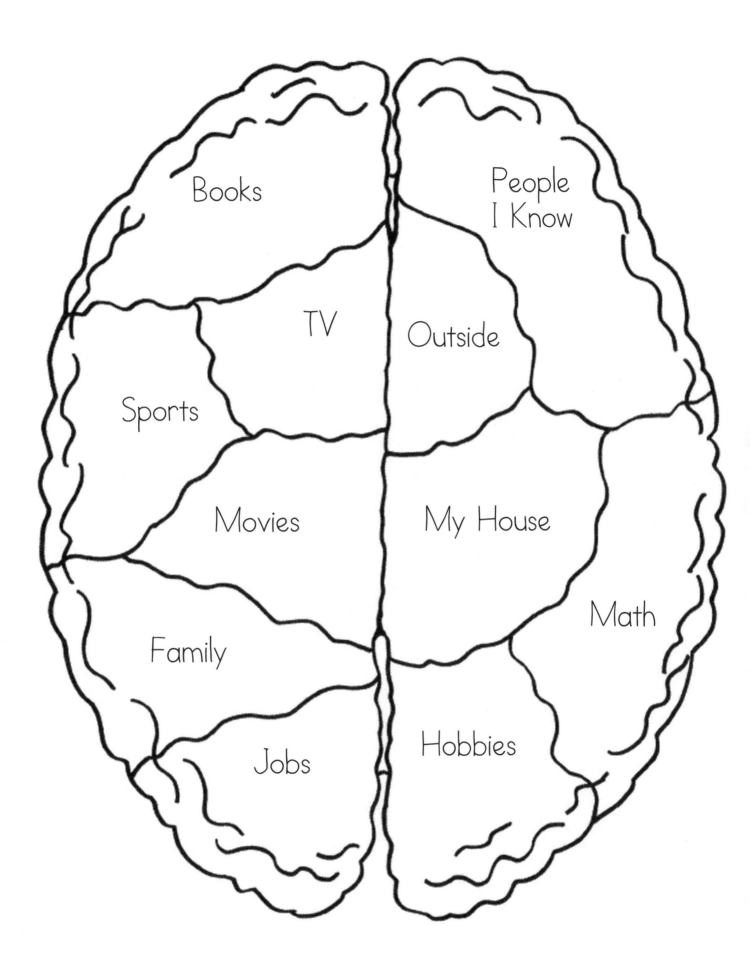

BEST PRACTICE

Determining Importance

Researchers at the University of California at Berkeley have estimated that the amount of data available to us is actually doubling every few years. The advent of the Internet has dramatically increased both the volume of information we have access to and the speed with which it becomes available. The result is often referred to as "information overload"; most of us are now exposed to more information than we could ever process effectively. Our students need strategies to cope with that overload.

Effective readers, for example, use specific strategies to identify important ideas and details within a larger body of information. The skilled reader must be able to derive information without becoming distracted by excess (Fountas and Pinnell, 2001). For many students, the ability to focus attention on important information is a challenge. A student who has been diagnosed with Attention Deficit Hyperactivity Disorder (ADHD) experiences variability in attention that can frustrate even the most motivated child and teacher. Other children may have "shadows of ADHD," personalities that include many of the symptoms of ADHD, but not enough to qualify for that diagnosis according to medical standards. Students with shadows of ADHD may also have a difficult time determining important concepts that need their attention, especially when it comes to complex written material (Ratey, 2008).

Reflective Questions

- When learning, how do you focus on the key concepts or most important pieces of information?
- Why do some of your students struggle with determining the most important points in their learning?
- What strategies do you employ to help students focus their attention on key learning?

Idea for Daily Practice

Bull's Eye

"I started using this at home, and it helps me get my homework done faster so I can watch TV." –EunJi J.

We expect students to absorb a large amount of information throughout the school day. They may be asked to listen to lectures and announcements, watch videos, participate in group discussions, and read from several different texts with several different purposes. Teachers understand that some of this information is meant to be mastered, while other information is provided at an exposure level—but are students always able to make that distinction? If students are to become more active agents in their own learning, they need to be able to determine the importance of information as it is provided to them, and again later as they are reviewing and studying. The Bull's Eye strategy, used in small or large groups, gives you and your students an opportunity to practice determining which information is important. The tactile and kinesthetic aspects of this activity help to engage student attention during the discussion and decision-making processes.

Materials

Reproducible #18

Sticky tack

How To

1. Choose a piece of fiction or nonfiction text appropriate to the students' reading level.

2. Make 5 copies of the reproducible, so that you have 20 darts. Cut out each dart.

3. Draw a large Bull's Eye on the board or on a chart pad. The Bull's Eye should include three concentric circles. Label the innermost circle "100," the next circle "50," and the outermost circle "25."

4. Apply a small piece of sticky tack to the back of each paper dart.

5. In class, have students sit in a semicircle around the Bull's Eye. Place the darts next to the Bull's Eye.

6. Point out the Bull's Eye and discuss the differing values of the circles. Relate this to the game of darts and the goal of landing the dart in the higher-value circles. Compare this to reading texts—noting that the goal is to pay extra attention to the most important points (those with the highest value) in a passage.

7. Explain to students that they will have the opportunity to identify important points in the reading by writing each one on a dart.

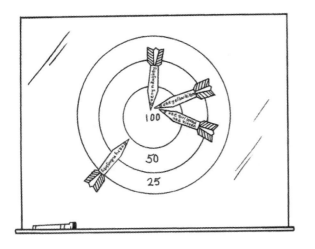

8. Begin reading aloud with the group. When a student comes across something she wants to write on a dart, pause and give the student time to select a dart and fill it in. Then direct her to place her filled-in dart on the Bull's Eye in whichever circle she feels best represents the importance or value of the information.

9. Continue reading, allowing students to stand and add darts to the Bull's Eye when appropriate. Eventually, the innermost circle of the Bull's Eye is likely to become crowded with darts, since students often feel that all of their points are very important. As the Bull's Eye fills up, engage students in a reassessment of the values of the various darts. Your questions might include, "Are there some darts that should be moved to a different circle?" "Now that we know more about the topic, are you changing your minds about the value of any information?" "How can we decide which are the most important pieces of information?"

10. Have students move darts into appropriate circles, discussing and justifying their decisions as they do so. When you finish reading the passage, ask students to think about the darts in the center of the Bull's Eye to see if those darts capture the most important information from the text. Point out how this information is a brief summary of the reading.

Additional Ideas

⚙ Copy the darts onto cardstock and laminate them. Students can then write on them with wet- or dry-erase markers. Darts can be reused after a quick wipe.

⚙ If the classroom has a magnetic board, attach small pieces of magnet tape to the backs of laminated darts, draw the Bull's Eye on the magnetic board, and proceed as above.

Reflections

How did the students respond? What evidence do you have that the strategy was successful? Are there adaptations to the strategy that you might try in the future? Other thoughts?

_____

_____

_____

_____

_____

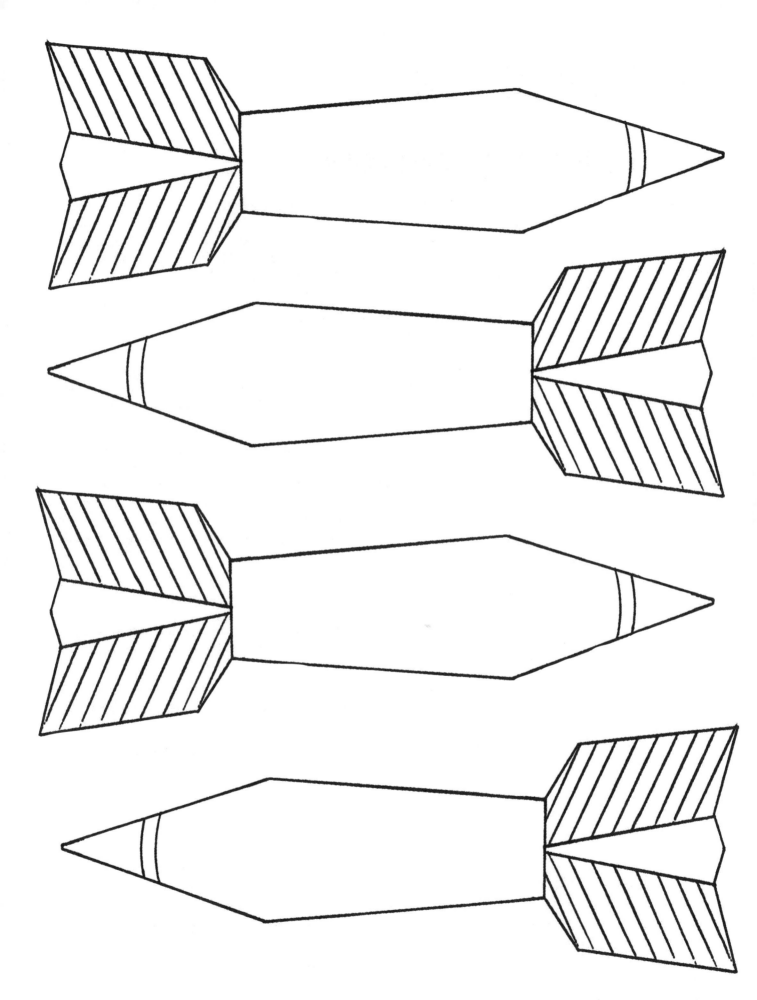

BEST PRACTICE

Strengthening Memory

The human brain is a complex organism, unique to each owner. The fact that each of us processes and retains information in different ways actually increases our chances of survival as a species. This is a good thing! But for classroom teachers, it can be a challenge to affirm each child's need to learn something in her own way. It seems faster to provide learners with a textbook definition or your own answer, rather than taking the time to have students generate their own thoughts.

But is that approach effective? Memory researchers suggest that the process of recoding information into your own language is one of the most important steps in developing a long-term memory of something (Sprenger, 2005). Recoding requires the individual to link new information with current knowledge—by choosing his own words, connections, or symbolic representations rather than relying on the teacher's. The process of personalizing leads to greater permanence.

In her book *My Stroke of Insight,* neuroanatomist Jill Bolte Taylor (2006) describes her personal experience with a massive stroke and her arduous journey to recovery. As a brain scientist, she was in a unique position to be very aware of what was happening to her and knowledgeable about what needed to take place for healing. She writes of her frustration as she tried to express herself and friends tried to supply her with the words she was searching for: "If I ever were to regain these abilities, then I needed to find that circuitry within my mind, in my own time, and exercise it."

Reflective Questions

- What strategy do you use most often for recoding information? Do you draw, make a bulleted list, reword, think in metaphors, or do something else?

- Which of your students seem to rely most on using your words or representations, rather than developing their own? How does this affect their learning?

- Which area of the curriculum might lend itself best to increased opportunities for recoding?

_____

_____

_____

_____

Idea for Daily Practice

Secret Code Books

> "Code books helped answer questions I would have kept in my head forever."
> —Dee K.

Academic language may be second nature to teachers, but it is like a secret code to many students. Because it may be different in structure and vocabulary than the language they use in typical social interactions or at home, it can be difficult for students to decipher. Secret Code Books tackle this challenge head-on by explicitly teaching students how to decode and recode academic language. Each student creates his own Secret Code Book and chooses from a menu of options for recoding. Because this activity allows each student to choose the recoding method that matches his learning style best, it improves comprehension and long-term retention.

Materials

Reproducible #19

Reproducible #20

Single-hole punch

Book ring for each student

How To

1. Make one copy of Reproducible #19 for every four students.

2. Make enough copies of Reproducible #20 so that each student has one copy for each new word being introduced.

3. Identify an academic term that may be new to students or that they may not have fully grasped. For example, while students may have heard the word *paragraph* repeatedly, some may not yet understand it or remember the key characteristics of a paragraph.

4. Pique student interest by explaining that teachers often use secret codes at school, and that it is up to students to decode the messages.

5. Provide each student with one cover page and an appropriate number of inside pages, plus a book ring for her Secret Code Book. Have each student connect the pages with the ring and then decode the message on the cover.

6. Lead students in writing the "secret word"—in this case, *paragraph*—and its dictionary definition onto a new code book page.

7. Explain that students will be expected to "recode" the secret word in at least two ways. Review each of the recoding options. Brainstorm ideas of how students might respond to each one in their own words. Be cautious about providing students with a visual example, as they may be inclined to copy exactly what you have done, rather than recoding in their own words.

8. When reviewing the analogy option, provide students with the first half of the expression. For example, for *paragraph* you might say, "*paragraph* is to *story* as. . . ." When developing these comparisons, reflect on the aspect of the word that needs greatest emphasis.

9. Later, make additional copies of the reproducible for the inside pages. When you introduce new academic vocabulary, have each student pull out his Secret Code Book and add a new page for each new word. Direct students to insert new pages in their books in alphabetical order so they can easily find specific words.

10. When an assignment includes one of the code words, remind students to pull out their Secret Code Books and review their understanding of that word. For example, if the assignment is to "Summarize the video on animal migration," students might refer back to their Secret Code Books to review the word *summarize*.

Additional Ideas

- At the end of the year, staple the book pages together and send the books home with students. Save the rings for next year's class.

- Consider coordinating with other grade level teachers, so that Secret Code Books can travel with students from grade to grade.

- For many students, the analogy option will be the most difficult. To make it more accessible, fill in the first three blanks. For example, you might write, "paragraph is to story as word is to _____." Or consider providing a complete analogy as a model and encouraging them to think of another example.

- For students at the secondary level, introduce the concept of coding with Reproducible #20 but without the Secret Code Books cover page.

Reflections

How did the students respond? What evidence do you have that the strategy was successful? Are there adaptations to the strategy that you might try in the future? Other thoughts?

_____

_____

_____

_____

Secret Code Book

Property of _____

Decode the secret message below:

R pmld blf xzm wl rg!

_____

A=z	J=q	S=h
B=y	K=p	T=g
C=x	L=o	U=f
D=w	M=n	V=e
E=v	N=m	W=d
F=u	O=l	X=c
G=t	P=k	Y=b
H=s	Q=j	Z=a
I=r	R=i	

Secret Code Book

Property of _____

Decode the secret message below:

Blfi yizrm xvooh ziv urirmt!

_____

A=z	J=q	S=h
B=y	K=p	T=g
C=x	L=o	U=f
D=w	M=n	V=e
E=v	N=m	W=d
F=u	O=l	X=c
G=t	P=k	Y=b
H=s	Q=j	Z=a
I=r	R=i	

Secret Code Book

Property of _____

Decode the secret message below:

R pmld blf xzm wl rg!

_____

A=z	J=q	S=h
B=y	K=p	T=g
C=x	L=o	U=f
D=w	M=n	V=e
E=v	N=m	W=d
F=u	O=l	X=c
G=t	P=k	Y=b
H=s	Q=j	Z=a
I=r	R=i	

Secret Code Book

Property of _____

Decode the secret message below:

Blfi yizrm xvooh ziv urirmt!

_____

A=z	J=q	S=h
B=y	K=p	T=g
C=x	L=o	U=f
D=w	M=n	V=e
E=v	N=m	W=d
F=u	O=l	X=c
G=t	P=k	Y=b
H=s	Q=j	Z=a
I=r	R=i	

Code word: _____

Defined as: _____

What it really means is:

_____

The secret is:

_____

What the teacher wants:

_____ is to _____ as

_____ is to _____ .

Looks like:

Code word: _____

Defined as: _____

What it really means is:

_____

The secret is:

_____

What the teacher wants:

_____ is to _____ as

_____ is to _____ .

Looks like:

Code word: _____

Defined as: _____

What it really means is:

_____

The secret is:

_____

What the teacher wants:

_____ is to _____ as

_____ is to _____ .

Looks like:

Code word: _____

Defined as: _____

What it really means is:

_____

The secret is:

_____

What the teacher wants:

_____ is to _____ as

_____ is to _____ .

Looks like:

BEST PRACTICE

Summarizing

Summarizing, the creation of a personalized account of new learning, is usually done in isolation. By its definition, it suggests that an individual must synthesize the input and develop a summary in his own words. But research on peer teaching, reciprocal teaching, peer editing, and cooperative learning suggests that interactive processing of information can lead to high achievement gains (Mitchell, 2007). In those situations, students working together have the opportunity to hear other opinions, compare two or more points of view, and justify their own thinking—opportunities that they do not have when working in isolation.

In most classrooms, students are encouraged to listen respectfully when a peer offers an opinion that is different from their own. Effective teachers also groom students to question intelligently, analyze any cognitive dissonance, and be attuned to any shifts in perception or understanding they might be experiencing. Some students need a few quiet moments for this type of reflection while others find that raucous debate sparks their thinking (Costa, 2008). You can accommodate both types of learners if you intentionally design your lessons with that goal in mind.

Reflective Questions

- In what situations do you find yourself checking your understanding of something by running your thoughts past someone else?
- How do your students respond when others have a different opinion or perspective? Do they listen? Become argumentative? Defensive? Passive?
- How do you ensure that students do their fair share when working in small groups?

Idea for Daily Practice

Instant Messaging

"It seems as though kindergartners know more about computers than I do!" Does this teacher's lament sound familiar? Many homes have computers available to their toddlers. And when children are exposed to computers from a very early age, technological skills become almost second nature to them. At the same time, most children are completely captivated by computers. Children who grow up surrounded by cutting-edge technology are excited when class activities incorporate the language, skills, or visuals of their technological world. The Instant Messaging strategy provides this excitement without the need for actual technology, tapping into student imaginations and the essential skill of succinct summarizing.

Materials

1 file folder for every two students in the class

Reproducible #21

1/2 sheet of blank paper for each folder

Tape or sticky tack

How To

1. Make one copy of the reproducible for every four students. Cut each reproducible in half.

2. Adhere one of the cut copies onto the top half of the file folder as shown in the illustration.

3. Ask students about their experience with instant messaging (IMing). Add to their explanations as necessary to point out:

   - Instant Messaging is typically used when two people are in different places so that they can't see each other or talk face to face.

   - When someone sends an instant message, that message usually takes the form of a brief phrase or sentence.

   - IMing begins with a short, quirky sound that indicates a message is coming in to the computer.

   - Each IM participant uses a screen name, usually different from his given name.

4. Assign partners and give each pair a file-folder "laptop," a half sheet of paper, and tape or sticky tack. Direct each pair to adhere the blank paper to the "keyboard" area of their laptop.

5. Ask students to create short screen names for themselves. If desired, make this more challenging by suggesting that the screen names be related to the content that is being studied. Each pair of students should write their screen names at the top of their paper, with their given names in parentheses.

6. Invite two students to help model the activity. Have them sit on the floor, back to back. Tell the helpers to imagine that they are both in their own homes in front of their computers and they are going to IM each other about what they learned in class. Their objective is to develop a summary statement that they both feel effectively represents their learning.

7. Student #1 begins by writing a brief statement about the learning. He then passes the "laptop" to his partner while quietly making a quirky sound.

8. Student #2 reacts to the statement provided by adding other salient information, offering a different opinion, or rewording the statement to make a more effective summary. Student #2 makes a quirky sound as she passes the "laptop" back to Student #1.

9. After they watch the modeling, have each pair find a place in the classroom where they can sit back-to-back on the floor and begin IMing. Students continue passing a laptop file folder back and forth, Instant Messaging, until they feel that they have accomplished the objective of developing an effective summary.

10. Monitor the activity to determine when students are close to completion. Announce a two-minute, then a one-minute warning that students need to complete their work.

11. Have students gather as a whole group. Lead a discussion about which points from the lesson were critical and should be included in a summary. Ask students to share their summaries.

Additional Ideas

☼ If real laptops are available, use these for Instant Messaging! A paper copy won't be available as a permanent product, but the benefits of summarizing and reviewing will still be plentiful.

☼ IMing can be used for other multistep tasks, too. For example, if students are being asked for 10 examples of a certain concept (nouns, multiples of 7, characteristics of the 1920s), each student in the pair can take a turn listing an example until all 10 have been generated.

☼ Suggest that students IM each other to study for an upcoming test.

Reflections

How did the students respond? What evidence do you have that the strategy was successful? Are there adaptations to the strategy that you might try in the future? Other thoughts?

Instant Message

Student #1: Hey, let's work on this problem together.

Student #2: OK. You start.

Instant Message

Student #1: Hey, let's work on this problem together.

Student #2: OK. You start.

BEST PRACTICE

Challenging Thinking

Neuroimaging has shown that the amygdala, the center of the limbic system, is stimulated by pleasurably challenging tasks. This stimulation facilitates the brain's ability to process information (Willis, 2007). Moderate challenge stimulates the brain and leads to the use of higher cognitive centers. While educators write and speak prolifically about the need to challenge gifted learners, brain research would suggest that it is critical to challenge *all* learners, no matter their current functioning level.

Experienced teachers know that all students are most engaged when the learning task is balanced just right—between "so easy it's boring" and "frustratingly hard." With proper guidance, most students are enthusiastic about accepting tasks that present a reasonable challenge. Add a bit of unpredictability and choice and you maximize motivation and learning (Hong, Ivy, Gonzalez, and Ehrensberger; 2007).

Reflective Questions

- How do you feel when you are given a moderately challenging task?
- What behaviors do you see your students demonstrating when they are not challenged enough?
- During which activities might you be able to empower your students to make choices about the level of task difficulty that's best for them?

Idea for Daily Practice

Wow 'Em Challenges

> "Although I am already a good writer, this strategy challenged my brain to work harder."
>
> —Courtney O.

Writing lessons are often open-ended enough to allow students to work at various levels. However, we as teachers need to focus on this even more carefully when designing our lessons. One of the recommendations of the National Writing Project is that "Educators need multiple strategies for . . . addressing the diverse needs of student writers." Or, as other writing experts state, "We can no longer approach all writing with one set of criteria, assuming that one size fits all (Cooper and Odell, ed., 1999)."

The same concept applies even more strongly to mathematics lessons, which often don't include a lot of built-in differentiation. Strategic lesson design that incorporates writing or mathematical challenges can ensure that students at any readiness level will continue moving forward. Wow 'Em Challenges offer a simple way to have challenging tasks available on the spot.

Materials

Reproducible #22

2 baskets or other containers

1 wet-erase marker

Sticky tack

How To

1. Make six copies of the reproducible, so you have six pencils and six calculators. Cut out and laminate each piece.

2. Fold each pencil and each calculator in half at the dotted line.

3. Consider the grade-level standards for students in writing and mathematics, and then develop tasks that ramp up those expectations to a higher level.

4. Use the wet-erase marker to write one task inside each pencil and one inside each calculator. Place a small piece of sticky tack along the bottom edge; close the paper and press to hold it closed. Place the pencils in one basket and the calculators in another.

5. Show students the Wow 'Em Challenge Pencils and Calculators. Tell students that these will provide them with a chance to "wow" their teachers and peers. Explain that you will occasionally prompt a student to grab a pencil or calculator from a basket and follow the challenge he finds inside.

6. When a student chooses a challenge, she works independently to complete it and then shares her work with you at an appropriate time.

Possible Writing Challenges

* Add dialogue.
* Add a metaphor or simile.
* Use alliteration.
* Use all of the five senses in your description.
* Use foreshadowing.

Possible Mathematics Challenges

* Develop a word problem using today's math concept.
* Think of something you might invent that uses today's math concept.
* If you change the order of your math process, what happens?
* Look for a pattern in today's lesson.

Additional Ideas

* Develop tasks at three different levels and copy reproducibles onto three different colors of paper. Coordinate task difficulty with a specific color, so that you can direct a student to choose a pencil or calculator in a color appropriate to his readiness level.

* Generate clip art that represents your science or social studies curricula and develop it into a challenge tool similar to the pencil and calculator. For example, use a Wow 'Em globe in a geography unit or a microscope in science.

* Secondary students might be motivated by the concept of a lottery. Print the words lottery ticket on small slips of paper and write a variety of content-related challenges on the back sides of the slips. Place the slips in a container and have students pick lottery tickets.

Reflections

How did the students respond? What evidence do you have that the strategy was successful? Are there adaptations to the strategy that you might try in the future? Other thoughts?

Wow 'em Challenge

Math Challenge

C	%	=/-	÷
7	8	9	X
4	5	6	-
1	2	3	
0	.	=	+

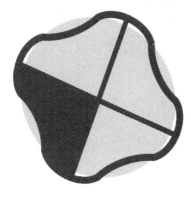

Fourth Quarter

BEST PRACTICE

Increasing Participation

Studies of the brain show that it releases dopamine, an essential neurotransmitter, in response to anticipated pleasure. Dopamine then takes an active role in heightening attention, improving executive function, and consolidating new memories (Willis, 2007). Luckily, we know that specific factors promote the release of dopamine in the brain; these include novelty, discovery, choice, and reward. Lessons that incorporate all of these will lead to high levels of student engagement and learning.

Reflective Questions

- What feelings do you encounter when you are anticipating a pleasant event?
- At what times during the week do you notice your students gladly anticipating a learning activity?
- What strategies have you used in the past to build anticipation? Can you use them more often?

Idea for Daily Practice

Pump It Up

Teachers often ask their students for more—a "thicker" question, a longer paragraph, a more comprehensive explanation, a "meatier" plot. The Pump It Up strategy incorporates a strong visual image for students to grasp when asked to develop stronger leads for their stories. A simple pump and a handful of colorful balloons immediately raise every student's sense of anticipation and motivation. Each pump of air inflates the balloon a bit more, helping students to understand why "more" is sometimes better. At the end of the lesson, two outcomes are obvious—a colorful starburst of twisted balloons and a large number of excellent story leads.

Materials

1 bag of long balloons (Remember to check whether any students have latex allergies.)

1 air pump (bike, balloon, or exercise-ball pump)

How To

1. Choose a component of the writing process that you want to reinforce; let's say you decide to focus on writing strong leads. Provide students with the characteristics of a strong lead. For example, you might teach students that a strong lead often incorporates novelty, movement, or emotion.

2. Test inflate a balloon in advance to check how many pumps it needs to be full.

3. Show students the deflated balloons. Explain that boring leads are often like deflated balloons—they are kind of flat. Leads that are pumped up with certain characteristics are much more exciting, as is a balloon that is inflated. Draw students in by beginning to inflate a balloon.

4. Assign students to groups of four or five and give each group a balloon. Explain that today each student will be writing a pumped-up lead. Groups are to help each group member develop a lead that includes novelty, emotion, or action. For each of those characteristics a student incorporates in his lead, he will have a chance to pump one burst of air into a balloon. The goal is for each group to have a well-inflated balloon.

5. When each group has had a chance to inflate a balloon, twist the balloons together into a starburst to celebrate the Pumped Up writing.

Additional Ideas

✿ Encourage students to come up with ideas for simple balloon shapes. Challenge them to describe how to twist the balloons to make the desired shape. This can make a great process-writing prompt!

✿ Consider other areas of the writing curriculum that could use some pumping up. You might ask each student to aim for descriptive writing that has at least three senses represented, a paragraph that has at least three details, or a poem that includes at least three metaphors.

Reflections

How did the students respond? What evidence do you have that the strategy was successful? Are there adaptations to the strategy that you might try in the future? Other thoughts?

_____

_____

_____

_____

_____

BEST PRACTICE

Focusing Attention

Low to moderate stress can actually encourage sustained attention (Jensen, 2006). When the brain experiences low levels of stress, it secretes hormones that direct attention to the source of the stress. While we don't want students to be "stressed out" in school, a little bit of stress might actually help keep them engaged. Stress that is teacher orchestrated—through activities such as questioning, debating, and other forms of competition—can hold the interest of those whose attention might otherwise tend to drift. When students know in advance that they might be asked a question about their learning, they develop a sense of accountability and thus tend to pay closer attention.

Students are also more attentive in classrooms where their knowledge is valued. In many classroom discussions, the teacher acts as the "primary knower" and students are "secondary knowers" (Berry, 1981). Teachers who are able to shift some of the role of knower to their students report seeing students who are more engaged, who demonstrate higher-level thinking skills, and who show a deeper level of comprehension (Aukerman, 2006).

As we give students the freedom to express their own answers, we must also give them the freedom to develop their own questions. According to Ruby Payne, an expert in the education of struggling students, "knowing how to ask questions yields a huge payoff" for students (Payne, 2008). This is especially true for those from families with little formal education. Students are able to master the academic language used for developing thoughtful questions when they hear that language repeatedly and have many opportunities to use it themselves. When you strategically build these opportunities into your lessons, you give your students the chance to hone these critical skills.

Reflective Questions

- How do you feel when you know you will be expected to answer a question in a group setting? What happens to your stress levels? Your ability to pay attention?
- How do you know if your students are paying attention during auditory presentations? What behaviors do you see?
- What topics lend themselves to shifting the role of "knower" to your students?

Idea for Daily Practice

Secret Questions

Most children enjoy having the opportunity to present their projects or learning to their peers. When several groups are presenting, often students enthusiastically raise their hands to volunteer to go first or next. It can be exciting to take the floor and be the center of attention; American artist Andy Warhol coined the term "15 minutes of fame" to refer to this experience. But his saying also referred to the lightning speed at which attention wanes. This can happen in classrooms, too. Frequently we find situations in which students are focused until they are not chosen, and then they lose focus. The Secret Questions strategy avoids that dilemma and encourages both the presenters and the listeners to stay focused.

Materials

Construction paper in green, red, and white

Markers

Staplers

How To

1. Cut construction paper into strips approximately 3 x 18 inches.

2. Assign students to heterogeneous groups of three to five. Provide each group with three strips of construction paper—one of each color—plus a marker and a stapler.

3. Direct each group to write "Secret Question" on their red strip of paper. Show a sample.

4. Inform students that today they will be presenting their group work to the rest of the class. To keep everyone paying attention, each group will generate a Secret Question about their content—a question that is answered by their presentation. To model this for the class, you might use an example related to a presentation on the solar system. The Secret Question might be, "How do we know the distance between the Earth and the sun?" Write this question on the green strip of paper, and write the answer on the white strip. Then staple the three strips together along the top edge, with red on top, green in the middle, and white on the bottom.

5. Monitor groups as they develop their questions and staple their papers together. Remind them to be sure that the answer will be provided in their presentation.

6. When the first group comes forward to make their presentation, hang their stapled strips of construction paper on the board or easel where they will be visible to the class. Remind the students to listen carefully to each group's presentation so that they are prepared for the Secret Question.

7. When the presentation is complete, ask the group to lift up the red cover strip, folding it back to reveal the Secret Question on the green strip. Encourage the class to discuss possible answers. When everyone is ready, have the group reveal the answer.

Additional Ideas

☼ Incorporate the Secret Questions strategy into video viewing or mini lectures to enhance student attention.

☼ Encourage older students to generate questions for which the answers must be inferred from the presentation.

☼ To mix it up a bit, have students generate a Secret Question that is open ended, without a single clear answer. (You'll need only two strips of paper!) Encourage students to justify and promote their answers.

☼ Switch things around by using Secret Answers. Following the presentation, each group provides classmates with the answer first, then has them guess the question.

Reflections

How did the students respond? What evidence do you have that the strategy was successful? Are there adaptations to the strategy that you might try in the future? Other thoughts?

Identifying Similarities & Differences

One of the most important skills students need to acquire to improve school achievement is the ability to identify similarities and differences (Marzano, Pickering, and Pollock; 2001). In a meta-analysis of the research on instructional strategies, researchers point to the clear advantages of being able to compare two or more concepts. The ability to make comparisons allows students to look for patterns and make connections, which then increases links between neural networks and boosts understanding and memory (Brooks, J. and M.; 1993).

Encouraging metaphorical thinking is one way of engaging students in finding similarities. This approach also has an added benefit: students develop fresh insights as they make comparisons between things that, on the surface, are different (Garner, 2007).

Reflective Questions

- Do you use metaphorical thinking (analogies, similes, metaphors, personification) to help yourself understand new concepts?

- In what ways do you currently use metaphorical thinking with your students?

- What are the instructional moments throughout the week that would provide opportunities to encourage metaphorical thinking?

Idea for Daily Practice

Metaphor Machine

A connection between fun and learning can motivate students to engage in higher-level activities such as metaphorical thinking. By adding a fun, tactile step to the creative process, the Metaphor Machine encourages students to develop metaphors. The Metaphor Machine is a symbolic yet concrete representation of the metaphor-development process. It shows students that when two ideas that seem dissimilar enter the brain, it's possible to consider their similarities and then restate those similarities in a metaphor, simile, or comparison statement.

Materials

Reproducible #23

Reproducible #24

Reproducible #25

1 cardboard box without a top and with a front approximately 8 1/2 x 11 inches

1 dowel, approximately 2 inches longer than the width of the box

1 roll of two-part carbonless cash register tape (available at office supply stores)

2 small paper cups

How To

1. Make one copy of the machine-face reproducible.

2. Make one copy of the nouns reproducible on yellow paper.

3. Make one copy of the verbs reproducible on green paper.

4. Glue the reproducible for the machine face to the front of the box. Cut a slit where the mouth line is located.

5. You need to create holes that the dowel can hang from. To do that, poke a hole in the horizontal center of each end of the box, approximately 2 inches from the bottom. Fit the dowel through one hole, slide the tape onto the dowel so that it sits inside the box, and fit the other end of the dowel through the opposite end of the box. Pull the two-part tape through the slit in the mouth, so that it is sticking out like a tongue.

6. Staple a paper cup to each end of the box near the top, as if the cups were in the place of ears. Make sure the open end of each cup is pointed up, so you can put pieces of paper in it.

7. Cut up the list of nouns. Place half the nouns in one cup and the other half in the other cup.

8. As the lesson begins, talk with the students about metaphorical language, defining what a metaphor is and what a simile is and sharing examples. Explain that we develop metaphors by taking two ideas, comparing them until we find a similarity, and then developing a phrase or sentence that brings them together through an unusual connection.

9. Show students the Metaphor Machine, explaining that it will help them develop metaphors and similes.

10. Take one noun from one of the "ears" and one from the other. Read the nouns aloud and encourage students to think of ways they might be similar. For example, if the words are *mouse* and *music*, students might recognize that they both make noise, they both might jump around, they both might be quiet, or they both might make people scream. Using the students' ideas, generate a metaphor or simile. For example, "after having thought that my mouse was dead, the sound of his squeak was like music to my ears" or "the violin music was mousey" or "the orchestra was filled with mice squeaking out a painful tune." Write the metaphor on the "tongue"—the roll of paper that is sticking out of the machine's mouth.

11. Explain to students that when they use the Metaphor Machine by themselves, they should keep one part of the two-part paper in their writer's notebooks (or their science notebooks, etc.), and then staple the second part to a bulletin board or scrapbook of metaphor examples.

12. Allow students the opportunity to use the Metaphor Machine during a writing lesson. Students may work individually or in pairs.

13. After students have had some experience with the Metaphor Machine, switch out the nouns to verbs. After further experience, load one cup with the generic nouns and verbs and the other cup with new vocabulary words from a unit of study (still using yellow paper for nouns and green for verbs). For example, during a science unit on Colorado wildlife, one cup might contain vocabulary words such as *elk, porcupine, mountain lion, migrate,* and *erode,* while the other cup could contain the original nouns and verbs. If a child picks a vocabulary word that is a verb, then he chooses a green verb card from the other cup.

Examples from Fourth Graders

⚙ Elk + i-Pod: "The elk bugled like an i-Pod."

⚙ Porcupine + rain: "The porcupine's quills can come out as easily as rain coming out of a cloud."

⚙ Mountain lion + fork: "The mountain lion's claws were as sharp as a fork."

⚙ Erode + hugging: "The sand is hugging the bank so that the water won't erode it."

Additional Ideas

☼ Students enjoy writing on the "tongue," but you can also adapt this activity to work without the dowel and roll of tape. Glue the Metaphor Machine face to a piece of cardboard, staple the cups to the cardboard as "ears," and staple the machine to a bulletin board. Tell students to write their metaphors in their writer's notebooks. Alternatively, you can just use two cups for the two sets of words!

☼ When students are learning a new vocabulary word in any part of the curriculum, pull a noun or verb card and challenge students to develop a metaphor or simile incorporating the new vocabulary.

Reflections

How did the students respond? What evidence do you have that the strategy was successful? Are there adaptations to the strategy that you might try in the future? Other thoughts?

_____

_____

_____

_____

_____

Rose	i-Pod	Music
Lion	Photograph	Pencil
Onion	Backpack	Time
Computer	Car	Jungle
Ball	Bike	Fire
Sandwich	Shoe	Fork
Pizza	Sweater	Road
Mug	Mouse	Toilet
Camera	Sofa	Cake
Book	Rain	Baby

Swimming	Crying	Singing
Driving	Sniffling	Cleaning
Talking	Hugging	Hammering
Eating	Stealing	Kicking
Writing	Worrying	Dressing
Sleeping	Thinking	Reading
Cooking	Sweating	Sneezing
Flying	Marching	Sewing
Coloring	Painting	Climbing
Saving	Running	Swinging
Screaming	Typing	Dreaming

BEST PRACTICE

Using Non-Linguistic Representations

The word *mnemonics* is derived from the ancient Greek word *mnemikos,* which means "of memory." One of the oldest memory strategies on record, mnemonics refers to a group of techniques that make links between words that are difficult to remember and visual representations or sounds that are easier to recall. Many of us remember learning the names of the Great Lakes through a popular mnemonic, HOMES (Huron, Ontario, Michigan, Erie, and Superior).

The research base on the value of mnemonic strategies is very strong. Meta-analyses of the research consistently show that the use of mnemonic strategies for all students results in a positive effect size. Studies also show that mnemonics are even more effective for students with learning disabilities (Mitchell, 2007). Can these strategies be made even stronger by adding a tactile component? Absolutely. When you link linguistic information with a visual representation, and then top things off with tactile input, you tap into the learning styles of all your students.

Reflective Questions

- How effective are mnemonics for helping you to remember things?
- What results have you seen when using mnemonics with your students?
- Which students need additional prompting to pay close visual attention?

Idea for Daily Practice

SNAP Shot

Digital photography is a medium that's familiar to many students. Many homes have access to either a digital camera or a cell phone with camera capabilities. Students know that the photographer looks through a view finder, carefully assesses the subject, focuses, zooms in or out to pick up key features, and clicks—creating a memory in print. Building upon this familiar experience, this strategy teaches students a process for focusing attention on key features of new learning and using a simple physical motion to lodge that new learning in the memory.

Materials

Digital camera (optional)

How To

1. If possible, show students a digital camera, using it as a hook to grab their attention. Explain that photos are often called "snapshots"—perhaps because they are a snap to take.

2. Write the word *SNAP* on the board. Tell students that the word *SNAP* is going to be a verbal cue for each of them to take a photo and paste it into her memory. Explain what the letters of SNAP stand for:

   S = Scan

   N = Notice

   A = Attributes

   P = Paste

3. Lead students in repeating the phrase "scan, notice attributes, paste" three times.

4. Present an example of something students are studying that lends itself well to the SNAP Shot strategy. For example, if students are learning the geographical features of their state, present a state map. Direct them to Scan the map. Ask them to Notice the map's Attributes while you cue them to look for specifics such as color, shape, size, and location. Have students share the features they notice. When studying literature, students might SNAP a plotline; in geology, students might SNAP the different layers of rock.

5. Ask each student to place her hands in front of her face as if holding a camera while looking at the map. Tell students that you will call out "one, two, three, snap," at which point each student should pretend to take a photo with her camera.

6. Direct them to close their eyes and imagine Pasting the photo into their memories.

7. Guide students in the use of the SNAP Shot strategy several times during the week so that everyone will remember the process. Then begin to prompt students to use it independently when the content lends itself to visual memory.

Additional Ideas

☼ To make the experience more powerful, shoot and print actual photos of the materials you are using.

☼ Allow each student time to sketch a SNAP Shot into her notes or into a construction-paper photo frame. Encourage students to use colored pencils or markers, which will enhance the visual memory.

Reflections

How did the students respond? What evidence do you have that the strategy was successful? Are there adaptations to the strategy that you might try in the future? Other thoughts?

_____

_____

_____

_____

_____

BEST PRACTICE

Making Connections

When they seek out precious gold and diamonds, miners go deep inside the earth. In a similar way, students must mine the depths of their brains in order to discover their rich learning potential. Although the brain works in very complex ways, you can present the process to students at any age level in ways they can understand. And when students understand how the brain works, they begin to value the mining process teachers ask them to undertake. Dr. Judy Willis, neurosurgeon and classroom teacher, suggests that students need to be knowledgeable about the brain. Students can be educated, she says, "to turn on their own neuroplasticity to build and maintain the neural networks needed to confront the challenges of a constantly changing knowledge base (2008)."

One of the things that brain researchers are sure of is that if the brain is to move new information into long-term memory, it must be able to connect that new information to data it has previously stored. The more connections the brain makes, the thicker the myelin sheath becomes. The thicker myelin sheath strengthens the neural pathway, which makes the new information more accessible for future retrieval (Sprenger, 2005). The strongest connections come about when a student develops his own personal, emotional connection to the content—but students can also derive additional value from listening to connections that others have made, and this process often prompts new memories and connections.

Reflective Questions

- How well do you understand the process your brain experiences as you take in information and store it for later use?
- What have you taught your students about how their brains work?
- How can you integrate information about the brain into your current curriculum?

Idea for Daily Practice

Brainy News

The Brainy News strategy encourages students to make connections between class work and the world represented in daily newspapers. Using newspapers allows students to discover connections between school learning and the broader world; it also sparks an interest in reading the newspaper. Each student can look for examples at her own readiness level, with some finding very concrete connections and others thinking in abstract, higher-level ways. Add to these benefits the fact that the Brainy News strategy requires very little teacher preparation, and it is sure to be a winner!

Materials

Reproducible #26

4-5 newspapers

How To

1. Before class, make a copy of the reproducible.

2. In class, describe for the students how information is received by the brain and how it must be connected to something else in the brain in order to be stored. Show students the reproducible, which illustrates how two brain cells communicate. Explain the process as follows:

   - A brain cell (also called a neuron) is composed of several parts.

   - Each brain cell has a cell body.

   - Branching off from the cell body in one direction are dendrites.

   - Branching off from the cell body in the opposite direction is the axon. At the end of the axon are axon terminals.

   - Dendrites receive information as a message that travels through the cell body, down the axon, and through the axon terminal.

   - At the end of the terminal is a gap, called a synapse, between the first cell and the next cell.

   - The information jumps across this gap in an electrical burst and attaches to the dendrites of the next cell, forming a connection.

3. Explain to students that the more connections a person is able to make, the quicker and smarter his brain becomes.

4. Provide students with a target concept from the material they have been studying. For example, in a geometry lesson, the concept might be "polygon." If necessary, do a quick review to make sure students understand the concept or meaning.

5. Pair off students or assign them to work individually.

6. Distribute sections of the newspaper to students randomly.

7. Direct students to glance through their newspaper pages to find anything that might connect to the target concept.

8. After sufficient time has passed, ask students to share their connections and record them on the board. Connections for "polygon" might include an advertisement for a cell phone that has a rectangular shape, football scores that remind a student that the shape of a field is a polygon, a corporate logo shaped like an octagon, or mention of a military meeting at the Pentagon.

9. Ask student helpers to collect the newspapers and store them for future use.

Additional Ideas

- Ask students to bring in used newspapers from home.

- Contact the major newspaper in your city or local community to explore opportunities for free newspaper delivery to your school.

- Have students cut out their examples and develop a bulletin board showing connections between the target concept and the daily news.

Reflections

How did the students respond? What evidence do you have that the strategy was successful? Are there adaptations to the strategy that you might try in the future? Other thoughts?

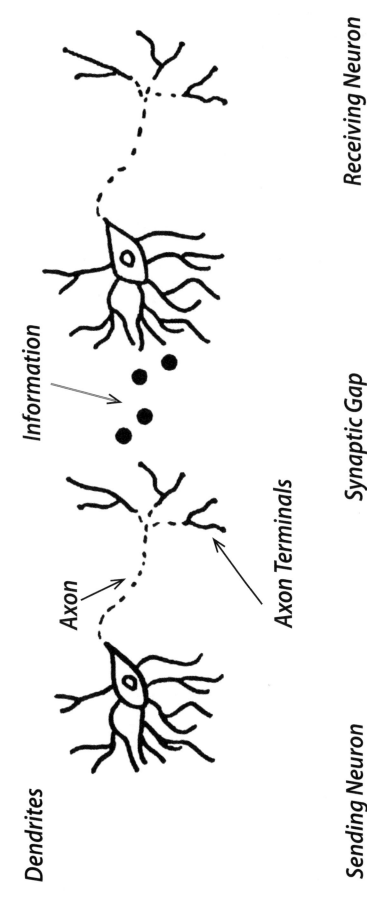

Dendrites

Information

Axon

Axon Terminals

Receiving Neuron

Synaptic Gap

Sending Neuron

BEST PRACTICE

Determining Importance

Conflict often has a negative connotation. Yet some researchers believe that "engineered conflict" can have a positive influence on learning (Jensen, 2005). When you intentionally design a lesson to include conflict—in the form of a structured debate, for example—you can often help students to synthesize new learning, determine importance, clarify their opinions, resolve discrepancies in understanding, and apply logical thought (Booth, 2006).

While some teachers may approach conflict with hesitation, the idea of a values discussion raises even more red flags. However, the reality is that students are immersed in values-laden situations on a daily basis, and they use their knowledge and skills to navigate and negotiate their way through these situations. Education experts suggest that in order to help students develop deep understanding, "the relevance of knowledge to one's own and other people's values should be a major topic of exploration in classrooms. This will increase students' interest in inquiry and also give them an opportunity to shape knowledge to their needs and circumstances and thus deepen it (Leithwood, McAdie, Bascia, and Rodrigue; 2006)." It follows that you should orchestrate classroom discussions that tap into the engaging nature of conflict and values, discussions that will develop essential cognitive skills.

Reflective Questions

- How are your thinking processes affected by discussions that involve strong, opposing opinions?
- When students raise conflicting opinions in class, how do you respond?
- Which sections of your curriculum lend themselves well to "engineered conflict"?

Idea for Daily Practice

Position Mixers

Many students have seen television scenes of their favorite musicians in recording studios. The technicians in the background are using mixers, synthesizers, and other recording equipment to find the perfect balance, trying to create that unique sound that expresses who the musicians are. With this mental picture in mind, students can understand the Position Mixer as a device for finding the right balance among various opinions or values. In addition, the hands-on nature of the tool turns a discussion that is auditory (and sometimes abstract) into a more engaging, concrete lesson.

Materials

Reproducible #27

30 brad fasteners or 30 small manipulatives (such as cubes, buttons, or pennies)

1 X-acto knife or other sharp cutting tool (optional)

How To

1. Make six copies of the reproducible; laminate the copies.

2. Cut along the dotted vertical line above each box on the reproducible. (If you have decided to use the small manipulatives instead, skip Steps 2 and 3.)

3. Insert a fastener into each slot.

4. Divide students into six mixed-ability groups. Provide each group with one Position Mixer.

5. Present your content for discussion and have the class identify five factors that relate to the issue. For example, if discussing the causes of climate change, students might list car emissions, factories, nature, media hype, and methane from cows. In primary grades, students might identify elements of caring learning communities, such as kindness, helpfulness, listening, following directions, and trying your best.

6. Direct a student in each group to write these factors into the boxes below the Position Mixer.

7. Explain to the class that each group is to discuss the value or importance of the five factors and use the slider (the fastener) to indicate their position. Clarify that a value of 10 is the highest possible, and a value of one is the lowest. (If using manipulatives, students position each object to indicate their choice.) Provide an example and demonstrate the task. Point out that differing opinions are expected and can aid in deeper understanding of the issue. Advise students that they should be prepared to justify their decisions.

8. Move around the room, assisting students as necessary to ensure that all are participating in the discussion and decision making.

9. After adequate time has passed, ask groups to share their positions. Have students share their feelings about the process, too.

Additional Ideas

✸ Make a copy of the Position Mixer for each student and explain that each person is to determine his position individually before working with his group. Each student can use a pencil and indicate his opinion by marking an X in the appropriate spot.

✸ Keep a laminated copy of the Position Mixer near the front of the room and access it for quick voting by the class.

✸ Make a transparency of the Position Mixer to use on the overhead projector with cubes or other small manipulatives.

✸ Design a large Position Mixer on a shower curtain liner and spread it out on the floor. Students can stand on the mixer to show their positions.

Reflections

How did the students respond? What evidence do you have that the strategy was successful? Are there adaptations to the strategy that you might try in the future? Other thoughts?

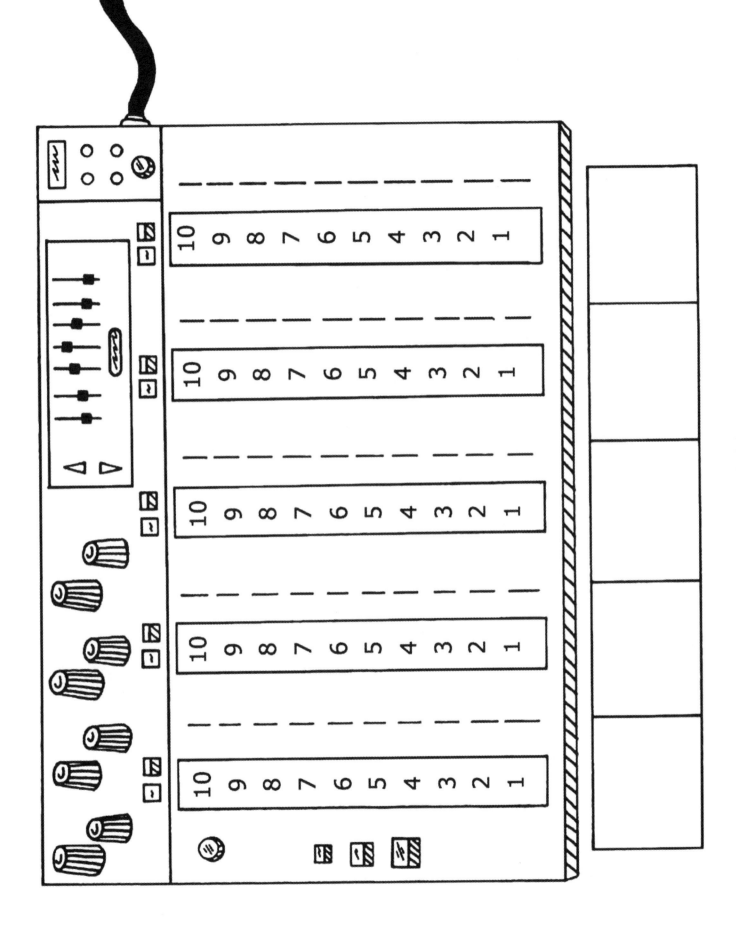

BEST PRACTICE

Strengthening Memory

The first step in getting new information into the memory is to grab the learner's attention. Lighting is often used to grab attention or to focus us on something important. Museums use spot lighting to enhance the beauty of art, while jewelry stores use it to highlight specific items in window displays. Lighting can increase the likelihood that something will be noticed by making it stand out from the busyness around it. In research done at the National Institutes of Health, scientists found that visual clutter actually suppresses the brain's responsiveness (Asher, 1998). Classrooms are filled with visual clutter, so teachers must find ways to direct student focus to key information.

Once a learner's attention has been focused, the new information must be saved in memory. Researchers suggest that the brain can retain semantic information more easily if it can link the information to a specific location. For example, if you post the five steps of the writing process on a classroom bulletin board in an ascending-stair design, students will have a location link to help them remember those steps. Even after the information has been removed, students who look at the empty location, or close their eyes and envision it, will be more apt to recall the information. This behavior, referred to as "spatial indexing behavior," allows for stronger use of memory (Richardson, 2008).

Reflective Questions

- How do you focus your attention on important items you want to remember?
- What things in your classroom are likely to draw the most attention? Why?
- How might you use spatial indexing to help focus attention amidst the visual potpourri present in your classroom?

Idea for Daily Practice

Flashlight Tag

> "Flashlight Tag made my mind work quicker to think of the answer. And it was fun!"
>
> —Jake C.

The allure of using a flashlight in the dark is familiar to most school-age children. It is reminiscent of camping in tents, being outside after dark, or reading under the covers after bedtime. Flashlight Tag taps into these associations, enticing students right from the beginning. More important, it shifts the focus of attention to a new location in the room. By tying visual representations and discussions to a specific, unusual location—the ceiling—you help students store their learning in long-term memory.

Materials

Marker

4 x 6-inch index cards or cardstock

Tape

1 flashlight for every five students

How To

1. Using a bold marker, write a vocabulary word on each index card.

2. Tape index cards flat against the ceiling in the area over the desks. Position them randomly, with a few feet of space between them.

3. Divide students into five small groups and give a member of each group a flashlight.

4. Tell students whether this is to be a cooperative group activity in which teammates can help locate the answers, or whether they are to function independently.

5. Point out the vocabulary words on the ceiling, reading each one aloud so that students have a sense of where each word is located.

6. Explain to students that when you turn the room lights off, they can turn the flashlights on. They will hear a definition or examples read aloud. For example, if one of the words is *gleaming,* they may hear a definition or a list of examples such as *gold, the sun, crystals, just-washed dishes,* and *polished silver.* The students holding the flashlights should quickly scan to locate the correct word and shine their lights on it.

7. Remind students not to be too quick to follow another student's lead. Just because someone shines his light quickly doesn't mean he's shining his light correctly!

8. Students within each group take turns passing the flashlight from one group member to another. In between turns, direct the students to face the lights downward on their desk tops.

Additional Ideas

☀ Write the branches of government on the cards and call out various responsibilities.

☀ Write numbers on the index cards and call out math facts. Students can shine the flashlights on the answers.

☀ Write states on the index cards and call out capitals or vice versa.

☀ On butcher paper, draw the steps of a process. Call out an example linked to a specific step in the process and direct students to shine the flashlights on the correct step. For example, in a unit on photosynthesis, a teacher might call out, "sunlight and chlorophyll make sugar." The students would point their lights at the correct step in the process of photosynthesis.

☀ Consider non-linguistic representations for Flashlight Tag. Symbols, colors, musical notes, pictures, dates, or portraits can all be used in Flashlight Tag to enhance memory.

☀ If flashlights aren't available, post the content cards on the ceiling over open areas of the room. Direct the students to stand under the correct answer and point up.

Reflections

How did the students respond? What evidence do you have that the strategy was successful? Are there adaptations to the strategy that you might try in the future? Other thoughts?

_____

_____

_____

_____

BEST PRACTICE

Summarizing

Summarizing, capturing the main points of something, can be a challenge for many students. Struggling students have a tendency to go on and on, giving you all kinds of unimportant details, without being able to succinctly capture the key information. All students need to be able to represent the information they have learned in a reduced form—and that involves not just remembering and under-standing, but also those higher-level thinking skills: analyzing and evaluating. While challenging for many, summarizing is an essential skill, with research show-ing huge gains for students who have acquired it (Marzano, 2003).

Summarizing is often assessed on standardized tests, and it is also relevant to everyday life. "Tell me what happened in 10 words or less" is a phrase used by teachers, bosses, parents, spouses—people in all walks of life. Our fast-paced lives don't always allow for lengthy explanations. Being able to choose key words to de-scribe the most important information clearly gives you a competitive edge when the clock is ticking. Quick notes to ourselves, lists of things to do, text messages to family—all of these activities of daily life require succinct summarizing.

Reflective Questions

- In what daily activities do you find yourself using just a few words to summarize a larger body of information?
- Which students tend to be too wordy with their responses? What might be the cause of this?
- What activities throughout the school day lend themselves to practicing brief summarizations?

Idea for Daily Practice

Google Key Word Meter

For a thousand years, the word *key* has represented a small metal device used to open a lock. But in more recent history, the meaning of the word *key* has broadened to symbolically represent the means of gaining access to knowledge, success, wealth, skills, and more. In education, it is common to talk about the keys to learning or the key ingredients of a successful classroom. In the past decade, the phrase *key word* has been introduced as a part of the Internet research process. Search engines require users to enter key words to search for information. When the user enters appropriately focused key words, the search engine responds with a more useful assortment of Web sites than when the key words are broad or inappropriate.

The Google Key Word Meter strategy uses the lure of the Internet to engage students in succinct summarization. As they work in groups to review content and generate the best key words for a search engine, students discuss salient points and evaluate the most important elements of their learning. By encapsulating their learning into a few key words for an Internet search, they receive immediate feedback and are able to evaluate the quantity and quality of the hits they get.

Materials

Reproducible #28

Several paperclips

Overhead projector

How To

1. Make one copy of the reproducible for each group.

2. Make one transparency of the reproducible.

3. In class, access a search engine such as Google on the computer. If necessary show students how to enter key words related to a topic of interest and then initiate a search. When the search engine has completed its process, it will list the Web sites it has found that match the given criteria; it will also note the total number of hits it has identified. Lead a discussion to get students' opinions on the value of a large number of hits versus a smaller number of hits.

4. Place the students in groups. Provide each group with a paperclip and a paper copy of the reproducible. Have each group place the paperclip at the X near the bottom of the page so that the clip can serve as an arrow on the meter.

5. Demonstrate how to use the paperclip with your transparent copy on an overhead projector.

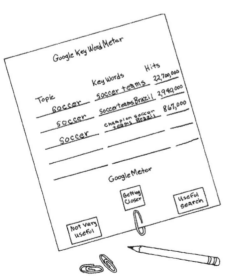

6. Choose a topic that the class has been studying and announce it to the groups. Direct them to write the name of that topic on the first line in the left-hand column.

7. Tell students to work with members of their group to choose key words that they believe will narrow their search to a useful number of hits. Have students enter these key words in the box in the appropriate column.

8. Use the classroom computer (or each group's computer) to check the number of hits the key words generate. Direct each group to write this number in the far right-hand column on their reproducible.

9. Lead a discussion about the results. Ask each group to determine the value of their key words and point their paperclip to the section of the meter that matches their conclusion.

10. Repeat the process, encouraging students to choose key words that will lead to a more effective search.

Additional Ideas

☼ Broaden the classroom discussion to help students see the application of key words to other learning tasks. Have the class brainstorm situations in which being able to choose the right few key words can be extremely helpful. Ideas might include playing games like Taboo, creating an e-mail subject line, text messaging, or writing a cartoon caption.

☼ If the class has access to individual computers, have students work on their own or in pairs to increase personal participation.

Reflections

How did the students respond? What evidence do you have that the strategy was successful? Are there adaptations to the strategy that you might try in the future? Other thoughts?

Google Key Word Meter

Topic	Key Words	Hits
_____	_____	_____
_____	_____	_____
_____	_____	_____
_____	_____	_____
_____	_____	_____
_____	_____	_____

Google Meter

Not Very Useful	Getting Closer	Useful Search!

X

BEST PRACTICE

Challenging Thinking

The availability of multiple forms of media in today's homes and classrooms is causing educators everywhere to take a closer look at what it means to be literate. No longer is it enough for students to be able to read books, newspapers, and reports. Successful students must also be literate in the visual, digital world. This expanded form of literacy calls for the ability to synthesize the meaning of visual representations and text for improved comprehension (McVicker, 2007).

Comic strips and cartoons combine visual representations and text to tell the cartoonist's story or point of view. The comic images grab children's attention and the humor of a cartoon can engage even the most reluctant student. Using comics has been shown to be a successful way to scaffold reading instruction for English Language Learners as well as other struggling readers (Ranker, 2007).

You can also use cartoons and comic strips to encourage creative thinking. Costa and Kallick (2000) believe that creating, imagining, and innovating are key "habits of mind" necessary for successful problem-solving. "All human beings," they write, "have the capacity to generate novel, original, clever, or ingenious products, solutions, and techniques—if that capacity is developed." Cartoons and comics can serve as models for creative thinking and as springboards for personal creative experience.

Reflective Questions

- Which comics do you find most engaging? Why?
- What opportunities do your students have for interpreting humorous visual representations?
- Are there specific students who appear to need greater creative challenges?

_____

_____

_____

_____

Idea for Daily Practice

Complete a Comic

Creating humor is a more complex process than developing expository material. To create humor, a student must be aware of what makes others laugh, and under what circumstances. In cartoons, the cartoonist uses text and visual representations to convey the humorous message to the reader. But what if the text was missing? The reader would need to interpret just the visual image and imagine the lost text. In doing so, the reader would most likely create new text, something different from the one the cartoonist had intended. The Complete a Comic strategy stimulates complex thinking skills by encouraging students to develop new text and humor.

Materials

Single- or multi-frame comics cut from newspapers or magazines

White-out

Cardstock

Wet-erase markers

How To

1. Before class, browse newspapers or magazines for single- or multiframe comics. Comics best suited for the purpose usually have simple graphics and no more than four frames.

2. White-out all or part of each caption. For example, you might choose to white-out just the punch line in the last frame. Glue the comic to a piece of cardstock and laminate it.

3. In class, show students an example of an incomplete comic. Together, brainstorm ideas for the missing text. Demonstrate how to write text in the empty space with a wet-erase marker.

4. Wipe off the sample text and place the laminated comics in an easily accessible place. When a student finishes her work early, prompt her to choose a Complete a Comic and develop text to replace the missing caption.

5. At an appropriate time, share the new comics with the class.

Additional Ideas

◉ During small-group time, introduce the Complete a Comic strategy and have each student work on his own comic.

◉ Encourage students to bring comics from home that they think would work well for the Complete a Comic strategy.

◉ Collaborate with the art teacher to teach students about cartoon drawing. Develop an interdisciplinary assignment in which each student develops her own incomplete comic for others to complete.

Reflections

How did the students respond? What evidence do you have that the strategy was successful? Are there adaptations to the strategy that you might try in the future? Other thoughts?

References

Allen, R. 2008. Analyzing classroom discourse to advance teaching and learning. *Education Update* 50 (2), 1–7.

Andreasen, N. 2001. *Brave new brain.* New York: Oxford University Press.

Armstrong, T. 2003. *The multiple intelligences of reading and writing.* Alexandria, VA: Association of Supervision and Curriculum Development.

Asher, J. 1998. *NIH News Advisory.* Retrieved October 13, 2008, from National Institutes of Health: http://www.nih.gov/news/pr/oct98/nimh-01.htm.

Aukerman, M. 2006. Who's afraid of the big "bad answer"? *Educational Leadership* 64 (2): 37–41.

Baumann, J., E. Kame'enui, and G. Ash. 2003. Research on vocabulary instruction. In *Handbook of Research on Teaching the English Language Arts,* ed. J. Flood, D. Lapp, J. R. Squire, and J. Jensen, 752–85. Mahwah, NJ: Erlbaum.

Beninghof, A. M. 1994. *Ideas for inclusion: The classroom teacher's guide.* Longmont, CO: Sopris West.

———. 1998. *SenseAble strategies: Including diverse learners through multisensory strategies.* Longmont, CO: Sopris West.

———. 2006. *Engage all students through differentiation.* Peterborough, NH: Crystal Springs Books.

Berry, M. 1981. Systemic linguistics and discourse analysis: A multi-layered approach to exchange structure. In *Studies in Discourse Analysis.* London: Routledge.

Booth, D. 2006. The role of literacy and literature. In *Teaching for deep understanding,* ed. K. Leithwood, P. McAdie, N. Bascia, and A. Rodrigue, 40–48. Thousand Oaks, CA: Corwin.

Boykin, A., K. Tyler, K. Watkins-Lewis, and K. Kizzie. 2006. Culture in the sanctioned classroom practices of elementary school teachers serving low-income African American students. *Journal of Education for Students Placed at Risk* 11: 161–173.

Boyle, J. 2000. The effects of a Venn diagram strategy on the literal, inferential, and relational comprehension of students with mild disabilities. *Learning Disabilities: A Multidisciplinary Journal* 10 (1): 5–13.

Bradbury, R. 1953. *Fahrenheit 451.* New York: Ballantine.

Brooks, J., and M. Brooks. 1993. *The case for constructivist classrooms.* Alexandria, VA: Association for Supervision and Curriculum Development.

———. 1993. *In search of understanding: The case for constructivist classrooms.* Alexandria, VA: Association for Supervision and Curriculum Development.

Brualdi, A. 1998. Classroom questions. *Practical Assessment, Research and Evaluation.*

Caine, R., G. Caine, C. McClintic, and K. Klimek. 2008. *12 brain/mind learning principles in action,* 2nd ed. Thousand Oaks, CA: Corwin.

Conklin, W., and S. Frei. 2007. *Differentiating the curriculum for gifted learners.* Huntington Beach, CA: Shell Education.

Cooper, C. R., and L. Odell, ed. 1999. *Evaluating writing: The role of teachers' knowledge about text, learning, and culture.* Urbana, IL: National Council of Teachers of English.

Cooper, E., and D. Levine. 2008. Teaching for intelligence: Parameters for change. In *Teaching for intelligence,* 2nd ed., ed. B. Presseisen. Thousand Oaks, CA: Corwin.

Costa, A. 2008. The thought-filled curriculum. *Educational Leadership* 65 (5): 20–24.

Costa, A., and B. Kallick. 2000. *Discovering and exploring habits of mind.* Alexandria, VA: Association for Supervision and Curriculum Development.

DiCecco, V., and M. Gleason. 2002. Using graphic organizers to attain relational knowledge from expository text. *Journal of Learning Disabilities* 35 (4): 306–320.

DuFour, R., and R. Eaker. 1998. *Professional learning communities at work: Best practices for enhancing student achievement.* Bloomington, IL: National Educational Service.

Fountas, I., and G. Pinnell. 2001. *Guiding readers and writers.* Portsmouth, NH: Heinemann.

Garner, B. 2007. *Getting to got it!* Alexandria, VA: Association of Supervision and Curriculum Development.

Gipe, J. 1978. Investigating techniques for teaching word meanings. Presented at the annual meeting of the American Educational Research Association, Toronto.

Goodlad, J. 1984. *A place called school.* New York: McGraw Hill.

Gregory, G., and L. Kuzmich. 2005. *Differentiated literacy strategies for student growth and achievement.* Thousand Oaks, CA: Corwin.

Gurian, M., and K. Stevens. 2005. *The minds of boys: Saving our sons from falling behind in school and life.* San Francisco: Jossey-Bass.

Guthrie, J., A. Wigfield, and N. Humenick. 2006. Influences of stimulating tasks on reading motivation and comprehension. *Journal of Educational Research* 99 (4): 232–244.

Hamann, S. B., T. Ely, S. Gafton, and C. Kilts. 1999. Amygdala activity related to enhanced memory for pleasant and aversive stimuli. *Nature Neuroscience* 2: 289–93.

Haynes, J. 2007. *Getting started with English language learners.* Alexandria, VA: Association for Supervision and Curriculum Development.

Hirsch, E. 2003. Reading comprehension requires knowledge—of words and the world. *American Educator* 10–29.

Hong, B., W. Ivy, H. Gonzalez, and W. Ehrensberger. 2007. Preparing students for postsecondary education. *Teaching Exceptional Children* 40 (1): 32–38.

Hord, S. 1997. *Professional learning communities: Communities of continuous inquiry and improvement.* Austin: Southwest Educational Development Laboratory.

Hyde, A. 2007. Mathematics and cognition. *Educational Leadership* 65 (3): 43–47.

Jensen, E. 2005. *Teaching with the brain in mind.* Alexandria, VA: Association for Supervision and Curriculum Development.

———. 2006. *Enriching the brain.* San Francisco: John Wiley & Sons.

Jones, S. 2003. *Blueprint for student success: A guide to research-based teaching practices.* Thousand Oaks, CA: Corwin Press.

Jorgensen, C., M. Schuh, and J. Nisbet. 2005. *The inclusion facilitator's guide.* Baltimore: Brookes.

Knight, D. 2006. *Teaching word meanings: methods that really work.* Atlanta, Georgia: International Dyslexia Association.

Leithwood, K., P. McAdie, N. Bascia, and A. Rodrigue. 2006. *Teaching for deep understanding.* Thousand Oaks, CA: Corwin.

Levine, M. 2007. The essential cognitive backpack. *Educational Leadership* 17–22.

Louis, K., S. Kruse, and M. Raywid. 1996. Putting teachers at the center of reform: Learning schools and professional communities. *National Association of Secondary School Principals Bulletin* 80 (580), 9–21.

Marzano, R. 1988. *A theory-based meta-analysis of research on instruction.* Aurora, CO: McREL.

——. 2003. *What works in schools: Translating research into action.* Alexandria, VA: Association for Supervision and Curriculum Development.

——. 2007. *The art and science of teaching.* Alexandria, VA: Association for Supervision and Curriculum Development.

Marzano, R., D. Pickering, and J. Pollock. 2001. *Classroom instruction that works.* Alexandria, VA: Association for Supervision and Curriculum Development.

McVicker, C. 2007. Comic strips as a text structure for learning to read. *The Reading Teacher* 61 (1): 85–88.

Mitchell, D. 2007. *What really works in special and inclusive education.* London: Routledge.

Ogle, D. 1986. K-W-L: A teaching model that develops active reading of expository text. *Reading Teacher* 39 (6): 564–570.

Paxton-Buursma, D., and M. Walker. 2008. Piggybacking: A strategy to increase participation in classroom discussions by students with learning disabilities. *Teaching Exceptional Children* 40 (3): 28–34.

Payne, R. 2008. Nine powerful practices. *Educational Leadership* 65 (7): 48–52.

Perkins-Gough, D. 2002. Special report: RAND report on reading comprehension. *Educational Leadership,* 60 (3).

Polacco, P. 1988. *The keeping quilt.* New York: Simon & Schuster.

Posner, M., and M. Rothbart. 2007. *Educating the human brain.* Washington: American Psychological Association.

Ranker, J. 2007. Using comic books as read-alouds: Insights on reading instruction from an English as a second language classroom. *The Reading Teacher* 61 (4): 296–305.

Ratey, J. 2001. *A user's guide to the brain.* New York: Pantheon.

——. 2008. *Spark: The revolutionary new science of exercise and the brain.* New York: Little Brown.

Richardson, M. H. 2008. When facts go down the rabbit hole: Contrasting features and objecthood as indexes to memory. *Cognition* 108 (2): 533–542.

Risley, B., and T. Hart. 2003. The early catastrophe. *American Educator* 4–9.

Scott, W., and J. Nagy. 2000. Vocabulary processes. In *Handbook of reading research,* ed. M. Kamil, P. Mosenthal, P. D. Pearson, and R. Barr, 269–84. Mahwah, NJ: Erlbaum.

Silver, H., R. Strong, and M. Perini. 2007. *The strategic teacher.* Alexandria, VA: Association for Supervision and Curriculum Development.

Society for Neuroscience. 2009. New studies show factors responsible for enhanced response to music. www.scienceblog.com/community/older/2003/G/20035362.html. Science Blog 2003.

Sprenger, M. 2005. *How to teach so students remember.* Alexandria, VA: Association for Supervision and Curriculum Development.

Stainback, S., and W. Stainback. 1996. *Inclusion: A guide for educators.* Baltimore: Brookes.

Tate, M. 2006. Learning styles. In *The Praeger handbook of learning and the brain,* ed. S. Feinstein, 289. Westport, CT: Greenwood.

Taylor, J. B. 2006. *My stroke of insight.* New York: Viking.

Wiggins, G., and J. McTighe. 2005. *Understanding by design.* Alexandria, VA: Association for Supervision and Curriculum Development.

Wilhelm, J. 2002. *Action strategies for deepening comprehension.* New York: Scholastic.

Willis, J. 2007. *Brain-friendly strategies for the inclusion classroom.* Alexandria, VA: Association for Supervision and Curriculum Development.

———. 2008. What today's neuroscience might mean for the classrooms of tomorrow. Presented at the annual conference of the Association for Supervision and Curriculum Development, New Orleans.

Wolk, S. 2008. Joy in school. *Educational Leadership* 66 (1), 8–14.

INDEX

Note: Page numbers in *italics* indicate reproducibles to be used with strategies.

Lesson accessibility, through Universal Design for Learning, 8

Levine, Mel, 59

Lighting, for focusing attention, 156

    in Flashlight Tag, 157–58

Lighting Up the Brain, activating prior knowledge with, 111–12, *113*

Listening, active, 59

Literacy, new meanings of, 163

Lottery tickets, Wow 'Em Challenges on, 129

M

Magic Prop Bag, for increasing participation, 15–16

Math

    background recordings for, 85

    Concept Continuum for, *26*

    Flashlight Tag for, 158

    Wow 'Em Challenges for, 128–29, *130*

    Writer's Revision Tool for, 19, *20*

Memory(ies)

    effect of emotions on, 28, 56

    paths creating, 38

    saving of, 36

    SNAP Shot enhancing, 146–47

Memory, Strengthening

    connections for, 148

    with graphic organizers, 38

        Spelling & Vocabulary Shapes for, 39–40

    with implicit learning, 82–83

        Spelling CD for, 84–85

    by recoding information, 118

        Secret Code Books for, 119–20, *121–22*

    with spatial indexing behavior, 156

        Flashlight Tag for, 157–58

Metaphorical thinking, for identifying similarities, 138

Metaphor Machine, for identifying similarities, 139–41, *142–44*

Mixed-ability groups, for Passing Time strategy, 47

Mnemonic strategies

    effectiveness of, 145

    SNAP Shot, 146–47

Motivation, making connections increasing, 32

Movement

    energetic students needing, 70

    in Human Machines strategy, 87–88

    for improving learning, 56, 66

    in Welsh Stomp, 57–58

Music, benefits of implicit exposure to, 82

Mystery Box, for creating connections to lessons, 90–91, *92*

N

Neurotransmitters, 66, 86, 105, 132

New ideas in education. *See also* Current initiatives in education

    criteria for evaluating, 6

Newspapers, for Brainy News strategy, 149–50

Non-Linguistic Representations, Using

    Flashlight Tag, 158

    graphic organizers, 70

    mnemonic strategies, 145

        SNAP Shot, 146–47

    during reading, 28

        Emoticons for, 29–30, *31*

    visualization, 105

        Director's Clapboard, 106–8, *109*

Note-taking, summarizing during, 41, 43

Novelty

    for grabbing attention, 14

    Magic Prop Bag for maintaining, 15, 16

O

Outdoor learning, for improving comprehension, 35

Outliers, 102

P

Participation, Increasing

    with active engagement of students, 94

        I'm In! poker chips for, 95–96, *97*

    with dopamine-releasing activities, 132

        Pump It Up, 133–34

    by grabbing student attention, 14

        Magic Prop Bag for, 15–16

    with positive feedback, 56

        Welsh Stomp for, 57–58

S